STEVE PARISH

AMAZING FACTS

ABOUT AUSTRALIA'S
HERITAGE

Text: Pat Slater

Contents

About Australia's heritage

Today the centre of Australia is desert, where rivers flow only after unusual falls of rain.

Human activity and introduced animals have reshaped Australia's landscapes.

An Australian Rules Grand Final at the Melbourne Cricket Ground is an all-Australian event.

The most ancient rocks on the surface of Australia were formed nearly 4300 million years ago.

Around 55 million years ago, the great Australian landmass finally broke away from Antarctica. In the ages since, the continent has drifted across the surface of the Earth, its plants and animals gradually taking on a distinctly Australian identity.

The Aboriginal people have lived in Australia for more than 60 000 years. Other groups have arrived in the past two centuries. Today, all Australians share a natural heritage consisting of the land, its plants and animals. They also share a heritage of all the things humans have made and done, from tools and buildings to systems of government and works of art.

Australia has a long and remarkable past. Today's Australians know the value of their heritage and do their best to make sure that future generations can appreciate it too.

Ruins at Port Arthur, Tasmania, date to convict days.

Kangaroos are well-known Australian animals.

Australia is noted for fine wool production.

Iron ore is a major Australian mineral resource.

A tall ship and historic warehouses are reminders of the past in modern Sydney.

About this book

This book is about people of many origins, and the ways in which they have interacted with each other and with the continent we call Australia. It is not intended to be a textbook detailing sequences of events, but rather a series of glimpses which may lead readers to make their own investigations into Australia's fascinating past.

The Index inside the back cover will give ready reference to the people and events included in the book. Words marked with an asterisk (*) in the text can be found explained and enlarged upon in the Appendix on page 79. Some further reading is listed on page 80, and your local library should contain many other interesting books.

We hope you enjoy these episodes in the journey of Australia and Australians through the years.

Aborigines look after much of their traditional lands.

Darwin, like other Australian cities, has a multicultural population.

Como House was begun in 1847.

A monument to failed hopes.

Aborigines cut bark from this tree to make a shield.

5

Discovering past and present

Discovering how people lived in the past

In order to discover what happened to humans in the past, historians may study:
- Human remains, usually in the form of bodies or skeletons, preserved deliberately or by chance.
- Things which show what people looked like and how they lived. These may include drawings, paintings, sculptures, photographs, films and videotapes.
- Things made and used by people who lived in past times, such as clothing, tools, weapons, buildings, furniture, writings, artworks, religious objects, toys and animal harness.
- Places used for special activities, such as growing crops, keeping or hunting animals, burying the dead, holding religious ceremonies, making tools or weapons, or competing in games.
- Records such as written histories, *biographies and *autobiographies, documentary films and writing on *monuments.
- Eye-witness accounts, hearsay stories, legends, folklore and songs.

John Simpson Kirkpatrick served in the Field Ambulance Corps at Gallipoli and rescued the wounded until he was killed. Historians have researched the man behind the legend.

Things people made and used

An *archaeologist learns about humans and their history by studying physical evidence such as things people made and used.

The age of an object may be discovered if it can be placed in a sequence of other objects whose dates are known. Radiocarbon dating, most accurate when dating things back to 25 000 years before the present (b.p.), can be used for charcoal, bone or other once-living material. Objects which have been subjected to great heat, such as fired clay pots, can also be dated scientifically.

History into legend

The historian tries to find out what really happened.

This is not always easy. In human interactions there are usually many points of view. Also, there is truth in the saying "history is written by winners".

As time passes, the facts about a person or an event may become distorted or forgotten, or the truth may be deliberately changed to make a better story. In time, such an improved story may be popularly thought to be the truth. This is how legends are born.

Squatters and swagmen, bushrangers and striking shearers, Ned Kelly and Henry Parkes, Gallipoli and Cyclone Tracy, Truganini and Jundamurra, Sir Donald Bradman and Sir Macfarlane Burnet – often the real story is even more remarkable than the legend.

History and legend are parts of a nation's heritage.

Marine archaeologists working on the wreck of the *Tryall*, the first British ship to sight Australia, wrecked off the coast of WA in 1622.

A timetable for humans in Australia

1986	Legal bond between Australia and Britain dissolved.
1976	Aboriginal Lands Right Act passed.
	Family Law Act came into force.
1975	Colour TV introduced to Australia.
1974	Cyclone Tracy destroys Darwin.
1973	18 becomes legal age to vote.
1972	Labor government recognises Republic of China; ends Vietnam involvement.
1971	First Green Ban protects Heritage area.
1967	Aborigines given voting rights.
1965	Australia sends troops to Vietnam.
1961	*Contraceptive pill available.
1956	First TV broadcast made in Sydney.
	Olympic Games held in Melbourne.
1945	End of World War II.
1942	Darwin bombed.
1939	Australia enters World War II.
1933	WA made to remain in Commonwealth.
1932	Sydney Harbour Bridge opened.
	Over 30% of workforce unemployed.
1931	*Depression - unemployment at 28%.
1918	End of World War I.
1915	Landing of ANZ troops at Gallipoli.
1914	Australia enters World War I.
1908	Canberra to be Australia's capital.
1901	Federation creates Commonwealth of Australia.
	First Parliament in Melbourne.
1899	Women given vote in WA.
1894	Women given vote in SA.
1892	Gold discovered at Coolgardie, WA.
1890-91	Depression. Foundation of Labor Party.
1881	First census - 2.25 million Europeans.
1877	Australia wins first cricket Test v. Eng.
1871	Australia linked to world by telegraph.
1868	Transportation of convicts to WA stops.
1863	First Pacific Is labourers brought to Qld.
1861	Lambing Flat attack on Chinese.
1861	First Melbourne Cup.
1854	Eureka Stockade battle at Ballarat.
1853	Transportation to Tasmania stops.
1851	Gold discovered in NSW and Vic.
1850	Victoria a separate colony from NSW.
	Convicts arrive in WA.
1842	Moreton Bay a free settlement.
1840	Transportation of convicts to NSW ends.
1838	Myall Creek murders and hangings.
1836	SA founded as independent colony.
1835	John Batman "buys" land on Yarra R.
1830	Prison at Port Arthur, Tas.
	"Black Line" fails in Tas.
1829	Settlement on Swan River (Perth), WA.

1825	Van Diemen's Land (Tas.) a separate colony.
1824	Convict settlement at Moreton Bay, Qld.
1823	First Legislative Council in NSW.
1814	Matthew Flinders suggests name "Australia".
1813	Blue Mts crossed, opening lands beyond.
1810	NSW Corps recalled, Macquarie Governor.
1808	Rum Rebellion deposes Gov. Bligh.
1803-04	Settlement in Tas. at Risdon Cove, Hobart.
1801-03	Flinders (*Investigator*) sails around Aust.
1798	Bass and Flinders sail around Tasmania.
1797	First *Merino sheep imported.
1791	Third Fleet brings Irish and other convicts.
1790	Second Fleet brings convicts and NSW Corps.
1788	First Fleet arrives with convicts, marines.
1770	Cook (*Endeavour*) sails up east coast.
1699	William Dampier (*Roebuck*) on WA coast.
1697	Willem de Vlamingh sails coast of WA.
1688	William Dampier (*Cygnet*) on coast of WA.
1644	Abel Tasman charts coast of Aust.
1642	Abel Tasman charts Van Diemen's Land.
1629	Wreck of *Batavia* on Houtman Abrolhos.
1623	*Arnhem* explores northern coast of NT.
1622	*Leeuwin* sights corner of WA.
	English ship *Tryall* wrecked on coast of WA.
1616	Dirk Hartog (*Eendracht*) at Shark Bay, WA.
1606	Luis de Torres sails through Torres Strait.
	Willem Jansz (*Duyfken*) lands on Cape York.
1522-24	Portuguese ships may have reached Aust.
1500s	Macassans begin voyages to NT for *trepang.
1405-33	Chinese junks may have reached Aust.
1200s	Aborigines in Vic. build stone huts.
AD	Anno Domini (in the year of Our Lord)
0	Birth of Christ
b.p.	before the present
3000	Aborigines use fishing lines and hooks.
4000	Dingo arrives. Small, specialised tools used.
10000	Returning boomerangs used in SA.
12000	Sea covers land bridge to Tasmania.
13000	Ice Age ends.
18000	Height of Ice Age. Humans living in Tas.
20000	Final survivors of *megafauna disappear.
25000	*Cremation of dead woman at Lake Mungo.
30000	Funeral ceremony used at Lake Mungo.
32000	Engravings on stone on Cape York Peninsula.
35000	Humans living in Warreen Cave, Tas.
37000	Humans living at Mount Mulligan, Qld.
38000	Humans living on Upper Swan River, WA.
40000	Humans living at Lake Mungo, NSW.
44000	Engravings on stone at Olary, SA.
50000	Humans in Arnhem Land, NT, create rock art.
60000+	Humans first appear in Australia.

From dinosaurs to megafauna

Australia sets off alone

The land masses of the Earth float on a liquid layer of molten rock. Over very long periods of time, they gradually drift and change position.

Australia was once far south of its present location, and formed part of the super-continent Gondwana. It shared rocks, plants and animals, including the reptiles known as dinosaurs, with Africa, India, South America and Antarctica. Around 100 million years ago, Gondwana began to break up. Around 55 million years ago (10 million years after the dinosaurs disappeared) Australia finally detached itself from Antarctica and slowly drifted northwards. It carried plants and animals, but no humans. At around the rate fingernails grow, it is still moving northwards.

Antarctic Beech trees are found in Australia's rainforests and also in other continents which were once part of Gondwana. *Inset:* The Koala once lived in rainforest, but as Australia became drier it adapted to a diet of eucalypt leaves.

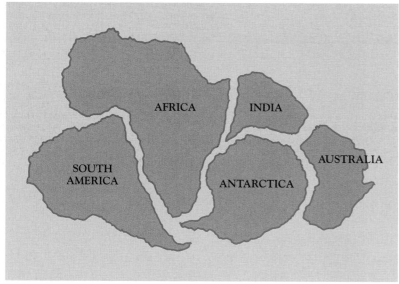

How today's continents could have once formed part of Gondwana.

The bigger they are ...

By the time humans arrived in Australia, more than 60 000 years ago, some *marsupials, birds and *reptiles had become very large.

Known as megafauna, these huge creatures included a monitor lizard scientists have named *Megalania prisca*, which was seven metres long and weighed over one tonne, and a six-metre snake with a head the size of a shovel and hundreds of teeth. The largest plant-eater was *Diprotodon optatum*, a wombat-like marsupial the size of a rhinoceros. One bird, *Genyornis*, looked like a huge emu and weighed up to 200 kilograms. Most megafauna groups were *extinct by 20 000 years ago.

The voyage of Ark Australia

On Australia's long journey, it went through cycles of warmer and cooler climates, with less or more rain falling. At some stages much of the inland was covered by shallow lakes or seas.

The plants and animals inhabiting the continent which adapted gradually to changing conditions survived. If they did not adapt suitably, they died out. Increasing dryness and generally poor soils favoured plants and animals which could make the most of food sources, survive poor seasons and breed up quickly when rains fell.

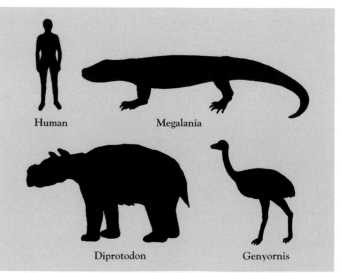

A human 178 cm tall compared with three members of the megafauna.

RECORDED ON THE ROCKS

Crushing ochre to use for painting.

Explaining the meaning of paintings.

A picture of a Short-beaked Echidna.

The Tasmanian Devil no longer exists in Kakadu, where its image is recorded.

Wherever Australia's first human inhabitants, the Aboriginal people, lived, they left records. Often these were pictures – engraved, stencilled, drawn or painted on rock. Some of these pictures recorded happenings in everyday life, or were done in play. Many were done as part of the religious or spiritual life of a group of people.

Pictures were often made on Dreaming sites, places where ancestral beings stopped on their journeys through the country and made things the way they are. The meanings of many pictures are no longer known. Sometimes there are still Aboriginal traditional owners of a place. They may still be associated with the pictures, and perhaps may be willing to tell outsiders something about them.

Paintings by Aboriginal artists are eagerly sought by art collectors. This is on bark.

Lightning Man, Namarrkurn, is said to make thunder with axes growing from his body.

A python sleeps beneath a gallery of rock art showing dreamtime figures.

Knowledge about paintings is passed on through the generations.

Making a hand stencil with ochre and water blown from the mouth.

THE PICTURES SHOWN ABOVE ARE PART OF THE HERITAGE OF THE ABORIGINAL PEOPLE OF KAKADU NATIONAL PARK, ARNHEM LAND, NT

DID YOU KNOW?

FACTS

▶ Sea level was 120 m below its present level about 52 000, and again about 70 000, years ago. Either time-window provided many years in which animals and people could enter Australia.

▶ Archaeological evidence shows that Aborigines were living in Arnhem Land over 60 000 years ago and had reached southern Australia by 40 000 years ago.

▶ The megafauna disappeared as the climate changed, creating deserts. Aboriginal hunting and seasonal burning of the land may have been other causes.

The first people on the continent

Some Arnhem Land caves were occupied for over 50 000 years.

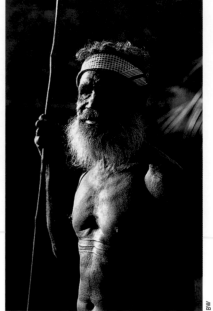
An Aboriginal hunter.

A new-found land

A generally accepted theory is that the ancestors of Australia's present-day Aborigines crossed to the continent from Asia before 60 000 years ago, at a time when the sea level was much lower than today.

When humans arrived, they discovered many unfamiliar animals, including the megafauna, with its giant *predators. By 20 000 years ago, there were people living all over the continent. They made tools and weapons from stone and wood, decorated rocks by carving or painting, made flour from grass-seeds, and wore skin cloaks and carved ornaments. They hunted large animals and fished, and gathered small animals and plant foods. They held ceremonies associated with important happenings, and there were rules of social life which governed the ways people behaved.

LIVING OFF THE LAND – SOME ABORIGINAL FOODS

Kangaroos and other *mammals.

Small animals and plant tubers.

Seeds, ground into flour.

Fruits and berries.

Fish, eels, shellfish and dugong.

Snakes, lizards and frogs.

Freshwater and marine turtles.

Bush honey.

Learning how a spear is made by watching.

Learning about the past by acting out a story.

Learning the group's way of life by dancing.

Many peoples, one land

In 1788, there were many groups of Aboriginal people, living in many different areas throughout Australia. Most of these people lived in small family units of between 15 and 30 individuals.

A number of these family units could be linked by a common language, blood relationships, marriage ties, shared ceremonies and shared responsibility for sacred places and objects. They would come together to make use of rich food sources during good years, or to share food during times of drought or flood. A seasonal food source such as Bunya Pine nuts might bring together a number of communities which normally lived some distance apart.

In areas with abundant food, in many places on the coast and along rivers, there were many Aborigines. In the desert, one small group might have to travel over a huge area in order to find enough food and water for survival.

The older men and women of a group passed its history, teachings and laws down to young people in the form of stories, songs, dances, and artworks on sand or rock. Loving care for children and respect for old people are traditional in Aboriginal cultures.

FACTS

▶ When Europeans arrived, there were about 126 tribal groups living in the NT. They spoke over 100 languages. In Central Australia, there were far fewer people and only a few languages.

▶ Songs were passed on, and weapons and ochre traded over long distances. Groups came together to harvest special foods such as Bunya Pine nuts and Bogong Moths.

▶ Tasmanian Aborigines shared fire, even with their enemies.

SOME TRADITIONAL ASPECTS OF ABORIGINAL LIFE

Loving care for children.　　Closeness to the land.　　Art used to record and teach.　　Fire used to help hunting.

Tools made of stone.

11

An end and a beginning

For many years before Europeans explored the northern coasts of Australia, Macassan fishermen from the islands to the north sailed their praus to the coast of Arnhem Land. They camped there, collecting and smoking sea-cucumbers. These "Malays" traded goods, probably took some Aboriginal adventurers as far as Singapore, and left the tamarind tree, the Dingo, the *dugout canoe and foreign words in Aboriginal languages.

The Dingo is a wild dog.   A sea-cucumber or trepang.   A prau off Australia's northern coast.

"It's for their own good"

The British colonised Australia at a time when Europe's nations believed they could invade countries they saw as less developed than their own.

They felt they were bringing benefits, such as their own religion and way of life, to these countries. If the people resisted invasion, they were killed or driven into rough terrain. Their hunting grounds were taken over, the game destroyed, and they died of diseases to which they had no resistance. From their "empires", the colonisers gained raw materials, food to send "home", land, and cheap labour from the conquered people.

Sailors from the French ship *l'Astrolabe* and Aborigines celebrating a good catch of fish at Jervis Bay in 1826.

The dispossessed

In 1788, there may have been more than 300 000 Aborigines living in Australia. By 1830, perhaps only 100 000 remained.

Settlers took over Aboriginal homelands. Traditional ways were overturned by a new culture, which broke down the authority of Aboriginal elders and rewarded people adopting European ways. Direct conflict and disease killed many Aborigines. As time went by, Aborigines became a source of low-paid labour, on outback properties or as manual or domestic workers.

Once Aboriginal resistance was overcome, the colonial governments decided "protection" was needed. From the 1840s, many Aborigines were gathered into settlements run by government or church authorities. From the early 1900s, children who were part-Aboriginal were often taken away from their families and put into government institutions.

Aborigines today own some of the cattle stations where once they worked for low wages.

Towards the light

By the 1950s, Aborigines and Torres Strait Islanders were still without many legal rights, but their rights to citizenship, to equal pay for equal work and to their traditional lands had become matters of public concern.

Cathy Freeman, a great Aboriginal athlete, displays both the Aboriginal and Australian flags.

Sun arise

In 1967, a *referendum made Aborigines full citizens. In 1976, the Aboriginal Lands Right Act gave traditional Aboriginal owners the right to claim vacant or crown land.

Since the 1970s, Aboriginal and Islander peoples have gradually won the right to determine their own futures and to preserve their cultures.

Some Aboriginal people of today.

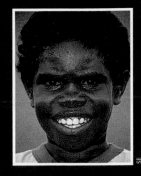

FACTS

▶ In 1838, at Myall Creek, near Inverell, NSW, white stockmen looking for cattle thieves massacred 28 Aborigines. Eleven stockmen were tried for this crime and 7 were hanged.

▶ In 1966, Aboriginal stockmen at Wave Hill Station, NT, went on strike for better wages. They were being paid $10 a week (a recent Federal award had set a wage of $23 per week).

▶ The special relationship of Aborigines with the land is now recognised in law and by other Australians.

FACTS

▶ Before refrigeration, spices such as nutmeg, pepper, cloves and mace were used to make salted, dried or rotting meat taste better when cooked.

▶ When voyages lasted months, seafarers ate salt meat and hard ship's biscuit (usually containing weevils). Symptoms of scurvy, bleeding gums and tooth loss, appeared after 68-90 days without fresh food.

▶ The Dutch East India Co. was formed in 1602. The largest of its 200 ships was 50 m long (a modern Manly ferry is 70.4 m). These small ships sailed from Holland 20 000 km around the Cape of Good Hope to Batavia.

Zuytdorp Cliffs were named after a Dutch ship wrecked there in 1712.

CHINESE, PORTUGUESE AND DUTCH NAVIGATORS

Tall ships sailing past

By the end of the 1400s, European countries such as Portugal and Spain were developing new methods of building ships, navigating, and charting. They wanted riches, spices, territory and Christian converts.

In 1488, Diaz reached the Cape of Good Hope; in 1492, Columbus crossed the Atlantic; in 1497-98, da Gama sailed to India; and in 1519-22 Magellan sailed around the world. De Torres sailed through Torres Strait in 1606, but Spain concealed the fact.

Holland claimed the spice-rich Dutch East Indies (Indonesia). During the first half of the 1600s, Dutch ships sailed west across the Indian Ocean with the *Roaring Forties for around 5300 kilometres, then turned north with the south-easterlies for the final 2400 kilometres to Java, in Indonesia. Captains who delayed turning north risked wrecking their ships on the coast of New Holland.

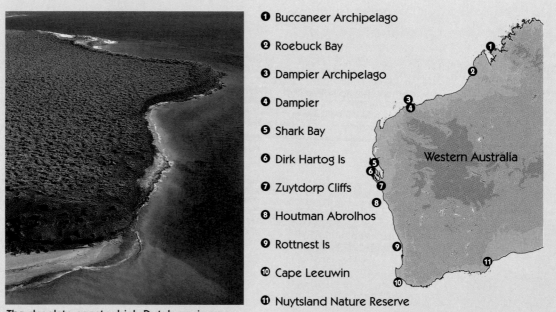

❶ Buccaneer Archipelago

❷ Roebuck Bay

❸ Dampier Archipelago

❹ Dampier

❺ Shark Bay

❻ Dirk Hartog Is

❼ Zuytdorp Cliffs

❽ Houtman Abrolhos

❾ Rottnest Is

❿ Cape Leeuwin

⓫ Nuytsland Nature Reserve

Western Australia

The desolate coast which Dutch mariners saw.

Dreams of gold

Stories of gold may have inspired the Chinese, Arabs and Portuguese to venture to northern Australia.

By 1400, Chinese of the *Ming Dynasty traded with Indonesia. From 1405 to 1433, Admiral Ch'eng Ho's junks made seven voyages of discovery to the China Seas. A Ming Dynasty statuette of the Chinese god of long life, Shou-Lao, found in 1879 wedged 1.2 metres below ground in the roots of a banyan tree in Darwin, may be a relic of a Chinese visit.

The Portuguese reached Timor after 1498, and Christovao de Mendonca may have explored Australia's east coast between 1522 and 1524. The Mahogany Ship, a legendary wreck said to have been found in the 1830s and lost after 1880 beneath dunes near Warrnambool, Victoria, is thought by some people to have been one of his fleet.

Despised by the Dutch

The Dutch who visited Australia were looking for lands which offered the opportunity for profitable trade. The coasts they saw appeared dry and, to them, useless.

Willem Jansz, commanding the *Duyfken*, landed on the west coast of Cape York in 1606. Dirk Hartog of the *Eendracht* landed on Dirk Hartogs Island, Shark Bay, in 1616, and left an inscribed pewter plate there. In 1697, Willem de Vlamingh took this plate and left another (*photo above*) in its place.

In 1622, the *Leeuwin* sighted the south-western corner of Australia. One year later, the *Arnhem* made contact with the northern part of Australia.

Abel Tasman discovered Van Diemen's Land in 1642, naming it after the Governor-General of the East India Company. In 1644, he sailed between Australia and New Guinea, then mapped from the Gulf of Carpentaria to North West Cape, sailed across the south of Australia and sighted New Zealand. However, the Company was only interested in gold, silver, spices and markets for trade, and Dutch exploration in the South Seas was discontinued.

WAMM

PAA

MUTINY, MASSACRE AND RETRIBUTION

A drawing of the massacre based on eye-witness accounts.

The salvaged stern of the *Batavia* today. *Inset:* A model of the *Batavia*.

WAMM

The Batavia, with 268 crew, soldiers and passengers, was wrecked on the Houtman Abrolhos in 1629. Captain Francois Pelsaert and 47 others set off in lifeboats for Batavia, 3220 km away. In their absence, mutineers led by Jerome Cornelius killed more than 125 men, women and children, hoping to seize the wreck's cargo of silver and escape in the rescue ship. Soldier Webbye Hayes led a group which escaped to another island then resisted the mutineers. When Pelsaert returned in the Saerdam, seven mutineers were tortured and executed. Two, Loos and de By, were marooned on the mainland, where Aboriginal people possibly adopted them and they may have left descendants. The rest were taken to be hanged in Batavia. The wreck was discovered in 1963.

Britain in the South Seas

Dampier identified the Banded Hare-Wallaby as "a Sort of Racoon" and noted that it was "very good Meat".

Australia's Black Swan was reported in 1636 by the Dutch ship *Banda*.

England began to make long sea journeys in the 1500s. Francis Drake's ships completed a voyage around the world in 1580 and the Spanish Armada was defeated in 1588.

During the early 1600s, European countries, including Britain, continued their search for new colonies, sources of goods and markets. By the late 1600s, it had become important, and fashionable, to study other lands and their inhabitants, and to investigate things such as the sea, the weather, the universe, plants and animals. During this period, England and France, who were traditional rivals, began to explore the South Pacific.

A bold buccaneer

William Dampier visited the northwest of Australia in 1688, on the pirate ship *Cygnet*.

He and the rest of the crew had abandoned their captain in the Philippines and gone looking for plunder. They were blown south from the China Seas and spent two months near the Buccaneer *Archipelago refitting their ship. Dampier wrote about New Holland in *A New Voyage Around the World*, published in 1697. Thinking New Holland might contain gold, the *British Admiralty made Dampier captain of the *Roebuck* and sent him to Australia in 1699. After landing at Shark Bay, the ship travelled northwards for five weeks. In 1703 Dampier published *A Voyage to New Holland*, which was eagerly read in Britain.

Dampier became so famous that Jonathan Swift pretended the hero of his book *Gulliver's Travels*, published in 1726, was Dampier's cousin.

A portrait of William Dampier by William Charles Dobson.

Dampier wrote that the Shingleback Lizard seems to have a head at each end.

Endeavour passing Queensland's Glasshouse Mountains.

The Glasshouse Mountains today.

A great endeavour

In 1763, Britain defeated France in the Seven Years War, and began to explore the far parts of the world.

Lieutenant James Cook *(right)* was told to take HM Bark *Endeavour* to Tahiti. After studying the planet Venus passing between Earth and Sun on 3 June 1769, he was to search for the southern continent. From Tahiti, Cook sailed around New Zealand, then charted 4000 kilometres of Australia's east coast north from Point Hicks, Victoria.

In four months spent on the coast, he made eleven landings, and named over 100 landmarks.

On the Great Barrier Reef, *Endeavour* struck a coral reef, was eventually floated off and spent 50 days at the Endeavour River, where Cooktown stands today, being repaired.

Cook made two more voyages to the South Seas, in 1772-75 and 1776-79. He sighted Norfolk Island and during each voyage made some contact with Van Diemen's Land.

Statue of Captain James Cook.

The cottage in which Cook's parents lived was brought to Melbourne's Fitzroy Gardens from Yorkshire in 1934.

FACTS

▶ Measurements taken when Venus crossed the face of the Sun enabled calculation of the distance of the Earth from the Sun. This was needed for more accurate navigation.

▶ Botanist Joseph Banks, two naturalists, two artists and two greyhounds (to chase game) travelled on the *Endeavour*. The mission: to study plants, animals and people.

▶ *Endeavour* was a converted coal-carrier, 32 m long, armed with 22 guns. She carried a milking goat, sheep, pigs and fowls.

▶ Cook made his crew drink lime juice and eat pickled cabbage, which they hated. This supplied vitamin C and prevented scurvy.

▶ When *Endeavour* ran aground, *Midshipman Jonathan Monkhouse suggested hauling a sail plastered with chopped rope, wool and animal dung under the ship. Water pressure held it against the hole in the hull.

17

Bound for Botany Bay

Sydney Harbour from the east side about 1800, depicted by the convict artist Thomas Watling.

In the late 1700s, harsh criminal laws resulted in overcrowded British prisons. In 1786, after using old ships as floating gaols, the British Government decided to take the advice of Sir Joseph Banks and establish a prison at Botany Bay.

Captain Arthur Phillip was to command the First Fleet of eleven ships. After the colony of New South Wales was proclaimed, he was to be its first Governor.

Eleven ships sailed for Botany Bay on 13 May 1787. One month was spent in Rio de Janeiro, another at the Cape of Good Hope, where cattle, pigs, goats, sheep and poultry were acquired. Phillip's advance party reached Botany Bay on 18 January 1788 and all ships were there by 20 January. It was decided that Port Jackson (Sydney Harbour) was preferable, and on 26 January the Union Jack was raised there.

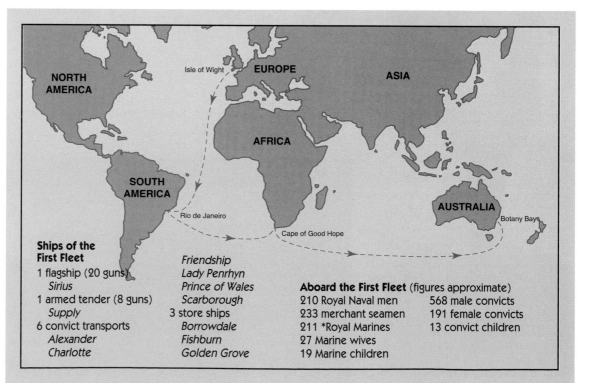

Ships of the First Fleet
1 flagship (20 guns)
  Sirius
1 armed tender (8 guns)
  Supply
6 convict transports
  Alexander
  Charlotte
  Friendship
  Lady Penrhyn
  Prince of Wales
  Scarborough
3 store ships
  Borrowdale
  Fishburn
  Golden Grove

Aboard the First Fleet (figures approximate)
210 Royal Naval men
233 merchant seamen
211 *Royal Marines
27 Marine wives
19 Marine children
568 male convicts
191 female convicts
13 convict children

The route taken by the First Fleet, the names of the 11 ships and the personnel aboard.

The starving years

The First Fleet brought only enough food to last the colony two years.

The soil at Sydney Cove was poor and seed rotted or failed to grow. The seasons seemed upside-down, stock died or wandered away. Convicts were unwilling workers and the Marines refused to supervise them. The Aborigines saw their lands invaded and their people killed and became hostile. Famine was relieved when the Second Fleet arrived in 1790. On it were over 1000 convicts and the NSW Corps to replace the Marines.

Captain Arthur Phillip, RN, by H. Macbeath-Raeburn.

Phillip returns to England

The Third Fleet arrived in July and August 1791, after 180 convicts out of 2000 had died on the way.

A tired, ill Phillip returned to England in 1792, taking with him the Aborigines Bennelong and Yemmerawannie. After his departure, the struggle for power between the NSW Corps, allied with the rich free settlers, and Governors Hunter, King and Bligh lasted for 17 years.

Cadman's Cottage, built in the Rocks district in 1815, is today Sydney's oldest building.

A view of Sydney today. The Opera House stands on Bennelong Point, with Sydney Cove and the Rocks district to its right. Behind the Opera House are the Royal Botanic Gardens and Government House.

FACTS

▸ 267 convicts died while at sea on the voyage of the Second Fleet, and at least 84 more died soon after landing.

▸ Ex-convicts were granted land (75 ha for a single man, 50 ha more on marriage, 25 ha for each child).

▸ The Port Jackson Aborigines noted that, like them, Phillip had a missing front tooth. Phillip was speared in the shoulder while making contact with Bennelong's group. The Aborigines offered to punish the thrower.

▸ Bennelong spent three years in England. He returned to Sydney and died in 1813.

▸ Good soil was found at Rose Hill. James Ruse, the first convict to receive land, soon grew wheat and maize there. In 1791, Phillip announced Rose Hill was to be known once again by its Aboriginal name of Parramatta, meaning "the place where eels lie down", or "head of the river".

19

▶ **THEY RULED NSW**

Phillip	1788-1792
NSW Corps	1792-1795
Hunter	1795-1800
King	1800-1806
Bligh	1806-1808
Macquarie	1809-1822

▶ Bligh had sailed with Cook, commanded a warship and, after the mutiny of the *Bounty* crew, had navigated 6400 km in an open boat, without maps, to bring his men to Timor.

▶ While Macarthur was kept in England after the Rum Rebellion, his able wife Elizabeth Macarthur managed the farms and brought up the seven Macarthur children.

Rum and rebellion

For 17 years, the colony of New South Wales was run by a group of officers of the NSW Corps and a few rich settlers, led by ex-Corps member John Macarthur. After Phillip left, Major Grose of the Corps was in charge for two years. Then Governors Hunter and King did their best to oppose the Corps but failed.

When Governor William Bligh arrived in 1806, he was under orders to put an end to a system in which a favoured group was granted land and convict labour, had free use of government stores, and traded in goods bought from visiting ships. Rum, which this group sold at up to 1000% profit, had become the "money" of the colony. The "Rum Corps" also controlled the courts.

Captain Bligh was a short-tempered man with a strong belief in discipline. He clashed with Macarthur several times and eventually arrested him. On 26 January 1808, the NSW Corps commander, Major Johnston, had Macarthur released. In a "rum rebellion", Bligh was arrested and imprisoned at Government House for a year. His attempts to gain support in Sydney and in Tasmania failed, and he returned to England, in convoy with the NSW Corps, after Governor Macquarie arrived.

A modern replica of *HMS Bounty*.

Father of woollies

In 1794, the colony's sheep were small, with poor fleece. Macarthur bred fine-woolled Spanish Merinos with animals which produced meat and coarse wool.

Sent to England in 1802 after fighting a duel, he resigned from the Corps and returned with a grant of land, which he named Camden, and merinos from the Royal Stud. After the Rum Rebellion he was kept in England for eight years, returning in 1817. During his absence, new pastures were found over the Blue Mountains. Macarthur and others sold their wool to English mills which supplied the flourishing British Empire with cloth.

A flock of Merinos. *Inset:* Elizabeth and John Macarthur.

Macquarie the builder

Macquarie Lighthouse, designed by Greenway.

Governor Lachlan Macquarie brought his own regiment, the 73rd Highlanders, to back him when he took up duties in 1809.

Free of the NSW Corps, he restored law and order, closed many public houses, raised the price of rum by a duty on spirits and freed convict women who married. With convict architect Francis Greenway he planned an orderly, clean Sydney. He erected public buildings and built roads, and encouraged farming and exploration.

A PAIR OF YOUNG ADVENTURERS

Midshipman Matthew Flinders (21) and Surgeon George Bass (24) arrived with Governor Hunter in 1795.

They explored Port Jackson in a dinghy, *Tom Thumb*, and then ventured outside the Heads and south to Botany Bay. In 1796, in *Tom Thumb II*, they reached Lake Illawarra. Bass and six oarsmen rowed a whaleboat to Western Port Bay in 1797, and later told Hunter that Van Diemen's Land was an island. The following year, Bass and Flinders sailed around Van Diemen's Land.

From 1801 to 1803, Flinders sailed right around Australia in the *Investigator*. Bass left the navy. He sailed to Chile and disappeared.

The tiny *Tom Thumb*.

FACTS

▶ Bass was tall and strong, while Flinders was short and slight. The one-masted *Tom Thumb* was 2.5 m long. In 1814, Flinders suggested the name "Australia". In 1817, Macquarie asked the British Government to use the name.

▶ Bungaree, an Aborigine, sailed around Australia on the *Investigator*, and explored the northern coast with King in 1817.

▶ Macquarie believed convicts who had served their sentences should be treated as free settlers. Macarthur and the "Exclusives", who wanted cheap farm labour, disagreed.

Over the western barrier

In 1813, by following ridges instead of valleys, Gregory Blaxland, William Lawson and William Wentworth discovered a route over the sheer cliffs and rugged gorges of the Blue Mountains.

Later that year, drought made Macquarie send Surveyor-General George Evans westwards looking for new pastures. He crossed the range and reached where Bathurst is today. Macquarie instructed William Cox to build a road 246 kilometres long across the range. This was done in 1814-15, by 30 convicts (guarded by eight soldiers), using axes and other hand tools, one horse, six bullocks, and two waggons.

Sheer cliffs of the Grose Valley, Blue Mts.

Rugged Van Diemen's Land

The visits made by French ships under d'Entrecasteaux (1792-'93) and Baudin (1802) to the coast of Van Diemen's Land (Tasmania) worried the British Government, since Britain and France were either at war or on stand-by at the time.

Governor King was told that while visiting Sydney Baudin's officers had talked about settling Tasmania. King saw a threat to British whaling and sealing interests, and sent Lieutenant Robbins to Bass Strait, where he claimed King Island. In 1803, King dispatched Lieutenant John Bowen with convicts, marines and free settlers to claim the Derwent River estuary, which was a good place to hunt Southern Right Whales.

One month later, Lieutenant-Colonel David Collins was sent by the British Government to establish a convict settlement. He found Bowen's site at Risdon Cove unsatisfactory and named his eventual settlement, at Sullivan's Cove, Hobart.

This tribute to Dutch navigators is in Hobart.

After war with France broke out again in 1803, King sent Colonel Paterson to settle on the Tamar River. In 1806, the settlement moved to the site of Launceston.

Six years later, Hobart became the centre of government. The south developed a population of government employees, convicts and whalers, while the north, which had good soil, attracted free settlers. They established farms and industries using grants of land and convict labour.

A model of Old Hobart Town.

Richmond Bridge was built by convicts in 1823.

A view of Hobart today.

A human tragedy

The Aboriginal people walked to Tasmania across dry land more than 35 000 years ago. They survived at least one ice age which occurred around 18 000 years ago. When Tasmania was cut off, as glaciers melted and the sea rose about 8000 years ago, there were between 3000 and 5000 people on the island.

European settlers claimed the land, and killed any of the Aborigines who protested. The Aborigines fought back. In 1830, a "Black Line" of 2000 armed Whites tried to drive Aborigines into a trap at Eaglehawk Neck. They captured only two.

George Robinson persuading some Tasmanian Aborigines to trust him; Truganini is on right, with arms outstretched.
Benjamin Duterrau (1767–1851), The Conciliation, 1840. oil on canvas, 1210 x 1700 cm, Tasmanian Museum & Art Gallery

Disease and settler persecution had killed many Aborigines before George Robinson, a missionary who was aided by an Aboriginal woman from Bruny Island, Truganini, persuaded 300 people to surrender. By 1835, they had been exiled to windswept Flinders Island in Bass Strait, where most died. In 1847, the 47 survivors were sent to Oyster Cove, just south of Hobart. The last of this group, Truganini, died there in 1876.

In 1830, a prison for re-offenders was established at Port Arthur, on the Tasman Peninsula. Here convicts worked from dawn to dark in silence and were punished savagely for breaking rules. Sharks were common in the sea around, and savage dogs were chained across Eaglehawk Neck, the only land access.

Ruins at Port Arthur today.

Visitors are shown the savage dogs chained in a line across Eaglehawk Neck.

More than 1800 convicts were buried in unmarked graves on the Isle of the Dead. The prison at Port Arthur was closed in 1877.

FACTS

▶ George Robinson could not swim, and Truganini saved his life by pushing him across a river on a log to escape aggressive Port Davey Aborigines.

▶ Walyer, "the Aboriginal *Amazon", escaped from sealers in 1828. She led the Emu Bay people against the settlers, then died in captivity in 1831.

▶ Fanny Cochrane Smith recorded songs in a Tasmanian Aboriginal language around 1900. Tasmanian Aborigines are reclaiming their languages through a Language Retrieval Program.

▶ Today's Tasmanian Aborigines descend from people who avoided being taken to Flinders Is or who were living on Bass Strait islands.

An island rich in natural splendour

Tasmania received convicts for 50 years. From 1817 to 1824, under Governor William Sorell, steady progress was made. The island became a separate colony in 1825. Wheat gradually gave way to wool as a major export, but sealing and whaling flourished until the late 1800s, when few seals or whales were left. Resources such as timber, fishing and minerals were used to develop trade and industry, including shipbuilding.

The Thylacine (above), or Tasmanian tiger, was a striped, wolf-like, marsupial predator which failed to survive competition with the Dingo on the mainland. There were probably only around 2000 Thylacines in Tasmania when Europeans first arrived. The first recorded was killed by dogs near Launceston. Because they killed sheep, they were declared vermin, and the government paid over 2000 bounties in 20 years. The last known wild Thylacine was captured in 1933 and died in Melbourne Zoo in 1936. Possibly there are still survivors in some wild area of Tasmania.

The Death Flurry by Oswald Brierly (1817-1894) shows the red spout that told whalers the harpoon had penetrated the whale's lungs.

In the 1950s, the Tasmanian Hydro-Electricity Commission decided to harness the wild rivers of Tasmania's south-west. Against Federal Government wishes, the upper Huon and Gordon were dammed in 1972, drowning Lake Pedder. Conservationists rallied from far and wide to save the Franklin River from being dammed. The Federal Government stopped dam construction and passed laws to give it more power in conservation matters. In 1982, the Franklin-Gordon Wild Rivers, South West and Cradle Mt-Lake St Clair National Parks became World Heritage areas.

More about Australia's convicts

The first convicts sent to Australia landed in Sydney, in January 1788. The final 229 convicts landed at Fremantle, WA, in January 1868, aboard the Hougoumont.

The alternative to transportation was often hanging. Prisons just stored people before trial.

Hand irons at Wentworth Gaol, NSW

Irish "rebels" against British government were transported to Australia between 1800-1868 and Canadian political prisoners in the late 1830s.

Punishment for convicts who were found guilty of crime once transported included hard labour in irons, flogging and hanging.

Francis Greenway (1777-1837), convicted of *forgery, arrived in Sydney in 1814. He received a ticket-of-leave, then practised as an architect. After designing Hyde Park Barracks, he was pardoned in 1819. Under Governor Macquarie he designed or influenced the design of about 44 plain, elegant and functional buildings, including St James's Church and the Supreme Court in Sydney and St Matthew's Church at Windsor.

Over 80 years, about 160 500 convicts were sent to Australia. This number was made up of 135 800 men and only 24 700 women.

Convict labour was expensive to feed, clothe, house and guard. In addition, convicts were often unwilling workers.

Female convicts were seen as lacking morals and were often brutally treated.

A woman could live with a soldier or ex-convict, be assigned as a servant, or be put to work at the Female Factory at Parramatta.

Mary Reibey in her old age

Convicts who worked out their sentences were called expirees. Some were pardoned by the Governor (emancipists) or, like architect Francis Greenway, were given a ticket-of-leave to work for themselves.

Mary Haydock Reibey (1777-1855) was sent to Sydney in 1790, at the age of 13, for stealing a thoroughbred horse. At first assigned to Major Grose, she married free settler Thomas Reibey in 1794. She had seven children and, after her husband's death in 1811, efficiently ran the family business and was active in colonial affairs.

After the "starving time", Sydney's convicts were better fed than they had been in Britain. Many convicts went on to farm or set up businesses.

Most women made the best of their new lives. Some married, many raised families. Some were successful in business.

There are Australians today who with pride trace their family back to convict forebears.

Francis Greenway

On Yarra's banks

FACTS

► In 1803, David Collins was told to begin a colony on Bass Strait. He tried Sorrento, on Port Phillip Bay, thought soil and tides wrong and went to Tasmania.

► "Wild white man" William Buckley was a convict who escaped from Sorrento in 1803 and lived with Aborigines. He joined Batman in 1835, was pardoned, and died in Tasmania in 1856.

William Buckley

Batman makes his bargain with Aboriginal people near the Yarra River.

A favourable report on the land from Goulburn to Port Phillip Bay was made after Hume and Hovell travelled overland from Sydney in 1824. Tasmanians John Batman and Joseph Gellibrand applied to Sydney for land at Western Port Bay in 1827, and were refused.

The Henty family left Tasmania in 1834, settled at Portland Bay and by 1838 had established farms there.

In 1835, Batman "purchased" a large area of land from eight elders of the Dutigallar tribe for annual payments of axes, knives, blankets, flour and other goods. He decided to settle on the banks of the Yarra River.

John Pascoe Fawkner and his group landed from Tasmania in late 1835. Batman's group took the north bank of the Yarra, while Fawkner's settlers lived on the south bank. (Batman's group wanted the new town to be called Batmania, but Fawkner's favoured Pascoeville.)

Governor Bourke in Sydney was faced with an independent settlement which finally he had to recognise. In 1836, Captain Lonsdale, accompanied by soldiers and convicts, was sent to run the colony. In 1837, Governor Bourke visited, and presented a plan for the town of Melbourne. Superintendent La Trobe arrived to govern in 1839.

The Yarra River winds through modern Melbourne.

When the clipper Loch Ard was wrecked near Mutton Bird Island (inset) in June 1878, 52 lives were lost. Two eighteen-year-olds, seaman Tom Pearce and passenger Eva Carmichael, were the only survivors. Tom struggled ashore, then swam out again to rescue Eva, who had clung to wreckage for nearly four hours. He left her in a cave and climbed the cliff to bring help. Eva returned to Ireland, while Tom survived several more shipwrecks and eventually became a master of steamships.

The shipwreck coast

On the coast west of Melbourne, sealing and whaling were replaced by commercial fishing.

The Western Districts inland became known for fine wool, and coastal forests were cut for timber.

Shipwrecks were common on some parts of this coast in the 1800s. Today, tourists flock to coastal resorts and scenic areas. Access has been made easy by the Great Ocean Road, carved from the limestone cliffs by soldiers returned from World War I.

Towards the Great Divide

Sealers, whalers, timbercutters and farmers opened up Victoria's rich and well-watered south-east.

The area was named Gippsland, after Governor George Gipps, by Count Paul de Strzelecki, a Polish adventurer who explored the wild south-eastern corner of Australia in 1840. Gold was discovered in the 1850s, and later the huge brown coal deposits of the La Trobe Valley. Victoria's north-east includes the High Country of the Great Dividing Range.

An 1880s mountain mailman and his mail run.

A Cobb & Co. coach.

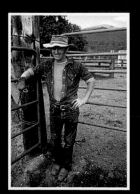

Stockman on Tom Groggin Station

▸ Bendigo, Victoria's greatest goldfield, had produced nearly 700 million grams of gold by the 1850s. The town was named after a brawling farmhand, who was nicknamed "Abednego", after a famous bare-knuckle fighter of the time.

▸ When exotic European dancer Lola Montez performed her Spider Dance at Ballarat, miners threw nuggets onto the stage. She horsewhipped a journalist who wrote her act was indecent.

▸ At Ballarat, before Eureka Stockade, about 500 miners swore brotherhood under a Southern Cross flag of white stars on a blue field, and burned their mining licences.

▸ Victoria's population increased sevenfold from 1851 to 1861. In 1877, Victoria had a population of 818 935 (NSW had 642 845).

▸ Melbourne was the fastest-growing city in the world in the 1860s. However, the city did not have a sewerage system until the 1890s and a few sensitive people called it "Smelbourne".

Gold! Gold! Hooray!

Gold was discovered near Ballarat, then near Bendigo, in 1851 and started one of the world's great gold-rushes. Miners flocked from all over the world, to pan for gold from creeks or to sink shafts up to 50 metres deep.

If they struck gold, they sold most of it to the government. Shipments were carted to Melbourne under armed escort for fear of bushrangers. The gold-rushes brought large amounts of money into Victoria. Business, trade and construction boomed. Demand for wool, wheat and other farm products grew. Ex-miners wanted a share in political power, and urged that each man should vote to elect the men who governed the colony.

Eureka Stockade

Miners objected to the government licence of 30 shillings per miner per month, and to licence hunts carried out by goldfields police.

In 1854, after soldiers arrived at the goldfields, miners led by Peter Lalor swore brotherhood and built a rough stockade. Police and soldiers attacked at three o'clock on a Sunday morning. The miners lost the 20-minute battle, which left 34 miners and six soldiers dead. Two onlookers were killed by police. About 100 miners were arrested, but were found not guilty of *treason. Licences were replaced by Miner's Rights, which carried the right to vote. Lalor, who lost an arm, later became a Member of Parliament.

Troops storm Eureka Stockade in 1854, overwhelming poorly armed miners.

Prejudice against the Chinese

The hardest workers on the goldfields were often Chinese, who stayed in their own groups and usually sent the gold they found back to their families in China. Many other miners became prejudiced against them and there were racist riots at Bendigo in 1854, and also at other goldfields. Many Chinese remained in Australia and became respected members of communities.

A one-armed Peter Lalor in 1856, portrayed by Ludwig Becker.

The hanging of Ned Kelly at Melbourne Gaol. *Inset:* The armour worn by Ned Kelly when captured.

In 1878, four policemen set out to arrest Ned and Dan Kelly, Joe Byrne and Steve Hart for stealing horses and cattle. Ned Kelly killed three of the four. The Kelly gang then robbed banks in Benalla and Jerilderie. Ned decided to derail a train bringing police to capture the gang, and in June 1880 the gang held more than 60 people hostage in the hotel at Glenrowan while waiting for the train. The police were warned; Dan, Joe and Steve were burned to death in the hotel and Ned was shot down in his homemade armour. He was hanged in Melbourne on 11 November 1880.

Gone feral

Victoria's bushrangers robbed and murdered travellers between Melbourne and the goldfields.

The first outlaws were usually desperate ex-convicts, but later ones were sometimes "wild colonial boys", looking for dangerous thrills as well as profit.

Bushrangers attacking a gold escort.

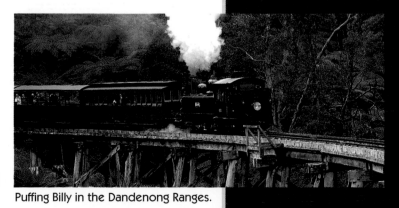

Puffing Billy in the Dandenong Ranges.

Moreton Bay Colony

The Old Mill was used for a time as an observatory.

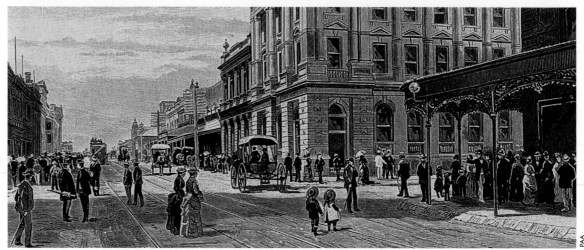

The intersection of Queen St and Edward St, Brisbane, 60 years after first settlement.

A severe settlement

In 1823, Governor Brisbane sent Surveyor-General John Oxley north from Sydney to find a site for a new, isolated settlement where difficult convicts could be punished severely.

The brig *Amity* landed soldiers and 29 convicts at Redcliffe in 1824. The settlement soon shifted to where central Brisbane is today. On 15 August 1826 Governor Brisbane proclaimed a penal settlement. Convicts were kept under very strict conditions, and for years free settlers were not allowed to live near Brisbane. The last convicts were removed in 1839, and the district was thrown open to free settlers in 1842.

By 1851, there were 10 000 people living in the "Northern District of New South Wales". The new colony of Queensland was eventually proclaimed in 1859, with Sir George Bowen as Governor.

Finding Pamphlett

The Old Mill on Wickham Terrace, Brisbane today.

The Brisbane River and Brisbane today.

NORTH TO CAPE YORK

In 1844-45, a party of seven led by Ludwig Leichhardt took 14 months to travel from Moreton Bay to Cape York, and then south and west to Port Essington, in the Northern Territory. In 1848, Edmund Kennedy and his group left Rockingham Bay for Cape York. After many hardships, only Kennedy and the Aborigine Jackey Jackey reached the Escape River area. Kennedy was speared by an Aborigine (right) and died in Jackey Jackey's arms. Jackey Jackey took 10 days to escape pursuit and reach the Cape. He led men from the ship Ariel back to recover Kennedy's body.

FACTS

▶ In 1859, there were 25 000 Europeans in Queensland.

▶ On Leichhardt's expedition, the great naturalist John Gilbert was killed by Aborigines.

▶ Jackey Jackey fulfilled his promise to Kennedy to carry his journals to safety. He returned to Sydney a hero.

▶ In 1863, the Jardine brothers drove cattle from Rockhampton to Somerset, near the tip of Cape York.

▶ Cooktown was established after gold was discovered in the Palmer River in 1873. It stands near where the *Endeavour* was repaired in 1770.

To the western plains

*Botanist Allan Cunningham reached the Darling Downs, 160 kilometres west of Brisbane, in 1827.

In 1828, Cunningham was the first European through Cunninghams Gap, which gave easy access to the Downs through the ranges south-west of Brisbane. By 1840, the Leslie brothers had "squatted" near today's Warwick.

Who were the squatters?

In all parts of Australia, "squatters" were people who settled on land without being granted rights to do so by the government.

These pioneers developed large areas of country and grazed sheep and cattle. Wealthy squatters had much influence with colonial governments and could be given title to their land.

The "Queenslander", a house raised on stilts, with wide verandahs, a breezeway and high ceilings, was developed to deal with heat, high rainfall and humidity.

Panning for gold in Queensland.

31

FACTS

▶ The 9 Archer brothers and their families settled the Fitzroy River basin, and the town of Rockhampton was founded in 1857. Townsville was founded in 1864, to service the cattle properties of northern Qld. Cairns was established in 1876, as a port for goldfields.

▶ The Prickly Pear came to Australia with the First Fleet, to feed dye-producing insects. By 1918, it had spread over 25 million ha of land, from the Hunter Valley of NSW to Mackay, Qld. In 1926, the *Cactoblastis* moth was introduced. Its caterpillars controlled the cacti and today the Boonarga Cactoblastis Memorial Hall, Qld, honours the triumph.

Forced labour

"Kanakas" were Pacific island men and women who from 1863 were brought to labour in Queensland's tropical north, usually on sugar plantations.

Often they were kidnapped (the slang term for this was "blackbirding"), or recruited with false promises. Men and women worked very hard under harsh conditions, they were treated poorly, their wages were low and many died.

In 1901, the new Federal Parliament, which was committed to cutting down the numbers of non-whites entering Australia, overrode the protests of Queensland and ended the system, after more than 57 000 people had been "recruited". In 1906, many islanders were deported. About 1300 remained in Australia, and today their descendants are valued members of Australian communities.

In the late 1800s the sugar industry depended on "kanaka" labour.

A "White Australia"

By 1888, all colonies except for Western Australia had introduced entry charges aimed at keeping out Chinese immigrants.

The unions were particularly concerned with lifting wages and living standards, and felt non-Europeans would accept the poor working conditions they were fighting. The Commonwealth passed the 1901 Act prohibiting recruitment of Pacific Islanders and the Immigration Restriction Act. Those who failed a dictation test in any European language would not be allowed to enter Australia. This began the "White Australia Policy".

Robert Towns, after whom Townsville (above) is named, brought in islanders to pick cotton on his property.

QUEENSLAND RAINFORESTS

Rainforest grows only where there is high and regular rainfall. Australia's rainforests existed when the continent was part of Gondwana, and they were widely spread for many millions of years. However, the continent grew drier and fires, which favoured competing eucalypts, became more common. By 1788, rainforests were common only on the eastern side of the Great Dividing Range and in Tasmania. Logging and clearing has cut them back to isolated stands. Today rainforests are priceless *reservoirs of plants and animals found nowhere else. They are visited by people from all over the world.

Green Ringtail Possum

Southern Rainforest Dragon

Rainforest needs high rainfall. *Inset:* Rainforest timber was one of Queensland's early exports.

A coral cay on the Great Barrier Reef. *Inset:* The Green Turtle and its eggs have long been taken for human food.

Under water on the Reef.

The tower built by convicts on Raine Island in 1844.

THE GREAT BARRIER REEF

The Great Barrier Reef consists of around 3000 coral reefs and 1000 islands. It extends along the coast of Queensland from the Tropic of Capricorn to Torres Strait. Long before Captain James Cook charted the Reef in 1770, the Aborigines harvested its food sources. In 1791, HMS Pandora, which was carrying some Bounty mutineers, was wrecked near Raine Island and over 1000 more ships were wrecked along the Reef in the 1800s. The Great Barrier Reef was declared a Marine Park in 1975 and placed on the World Heritage List in 1981. It is a great tourist attraction.

West coast settlement

DID YOU KNOW?

FACTS

▶ Captain Stirling wanted to call the Swan River colony Hesperia (after Hesperus, the evening star which could be seen in the west).

▶ Mrs Helen Dance, wife of the captain of the *Sulphur* and the most senior officer's wife not pregnant, struck a tree with a hatchet to symbolise the founding of Perth and the colony.

▶ Peel's settlers had little idea of pioneering. They took pianos and other luxuries instead of tools and supplies.

▶ About 400 Aborigines lived on the coastal plain near Perth. Stirling made no attempt to treaty with them. At the "Battle of Pinjarra" in 1834, Stirling and 24 others attacked about 75 Aborigines in revenge for spearings. One European and up to 50 Aborigines died.

▶ In 1832, the British Government decided land was to be sold rather than granted. Many left the colony (the Hentys went to Tasmania). By 1836, there were only 1600 colonists left. However, Perth had three breweries.

Mrs Dance prepares to strike a tree to declare the site of Perth, 22 km up the Swan River from Fremantle.
George Pitt Morrison, The Foundation of Perth, 1929, oil on canvas, 96.5 x 137 cm, Collection, Art Gallery of WA, presented by George Pitt Morrison, 1929.

The first settlement in Western Australia was made because Britain was afraid the French might claim it.

In 1826, Governor Darling sent soldiers and convicts under Major Lockyer to King George Sound. In 1827, Captain James Stirling explored the Swan River and persuaded Governor Darling it was a good place to settle. The British Government agreed – if someone else supplied the money. Thomas Peel formed a *syndicate to establish 10 000 people at the Swan River in return for land. In 1829, Captain Fremantle claimed the area, Stirling brought in the first settlers, then Peel landed 300 more.

Progress in the colony was slow. The rich settlers bought up all the best land, the soil was sandy and unsuited to European crops and there were too few labourers. The local Aborigines fought fiercely for their lands. By 1844, the colony was in such difficulties that the settlers asked for convicts.

An aerial view of Perth today shows the Swan River.

Captain James Stirling, RN

CONVICTS IN WA

Fremantle Museum, convict-built as a lunatic asylum in 1865.

Perth's convict-built Town Hall.

The first convicts arrived in Western Australia in 1850. No women were transported there and the men were not "hard cases". The convicts were treated much better than in the eastern States. They provided labour and, with their guards, were a market for food and other local products. Between 1850 and 1868, a total of 9721 convicts arrived in the colony. Transportation ceased in 1868, when the colony was doing well and had a population of 25 000.

Making tracks

After 1830, the Avon River valley met demand for farming land, and towns such as Northam and Toodyay were established.

In 1836, a track between Perth and Albany was made, and in 1842 Perth and Bunbury were linked. After convicts arrived, these tracks were upgraded to roads. By 1838, the colony was producing wool, whalebone, whale oil, wheat and oats.

Western Australia's wildflowers are world-famous.

A pioneer botanist

Georgiana Molloy arrived in 1830, and with her husband ran a dairy farm first at Augusta, then at Vasse River.

She collected and sent to England the first known specimens of many of Western Australia's native plants, often consulting with Aborigines as to their medicinal uses. Her work was used without acknowledgement by overseas scientists. She died at 38, after having her seventh child.

All Saints Church, Upper Swan, built in 1841 at the furthest point reached by Captain Stirling in 1827.

FACTS

▶ Convict-constructed buildings include Fremantle Gaol, Maritime Museum and Arts Centre, Perth Town Hall and the Barracks Arch.

▶ Busselton grew up around "Cattle Chosen", John Bussell's claim to land on the Vasse River, where he found a cow which had strayed 100 km from his Augusta farm.

▶ In 1876, when the steamer *Georgette* was wrecked near Cape Leeuwin, Grace Bussell and the Aboriginal stockman Sam Isaacs rode in and out of the surf for 4 hours rescuing survivors.

▶ A settlement south of Perth, Australind, failed but later became the port Bunbury.

▶ In 1871, Governor Weld reserved land on Mt Eliza, overlooking Perth city, as a public park. This area became today's magnificent Kings Park.

▶ John Septimus Roe, the first Surveyor-General, worked long and hard for the colony and died in Perth in 1878.

Eyre and Wylie were almost at the end of their endurance when they sighted the whaler *Mississippi*. Here Eyre is shown greeting Captain Rossiter while Wylie waits with the expedition's horses.

The golden West

In 1892, Bayley and Ford found *alluvial gold at Fly Flat, in the desert 560 kilometres east of Perth. By 1898, Coolgardie had a population of 15 000.

Paddy Hannan, Dan O'Shea and Tim Flanagan discovered surface gold 40 kilometres east of Coolgardie in 1893. Others later discovered one of the world's richest gold-bearing *lodes, on the Golden Mile. Gold was later discovered at Halls Creek in the Kimberley, at Marble Bar in the northwest and at Norseman, south of Kalgoorlie.

Kalgoorlie's streets were planned wide enough to allow a camel train to turn around.

Water for the goldfields

In 1903, a 560 kilometre pipeline bringing water from Mundaring Weir, near Perth, to Kalgoorlie (and also to the towns of the dry wheat belt region between) was completed.

Engineer-in-chief Charles Yelverton O'Connor, who had designed the pipeline and who had also been responsible for Fremantle Harbour, rode into the sea and shot himself ten months before the water came through. He had been the target of vicious attacks in parliament and the press.

Laying the Goldfields pipeline.

A canvas-suited diver seeking shell.
Inset: An opened shell might disclose a pearl.

Sea-gems and land-gems

Broome has been the centre of Australia's pearling industry since the late 1800s. In early days, pearl-shell was in demand for making buttons.

The first divers were Aborigines, Indonesians and Malays. From the mid-1880s, helmeted canvas suits were used. By 1903, Broome had a fleet of 300 pearling luggers, using mostly Japanese divers. It was a perilous occupation, whose dangers included sharks, cyclones and the *bends, a danger which killed 145 divers between 1909 and 1917. Plastic replaced pearl-shell buttons after 1945. Today, *cultured pearls are grown at Kuri Bay and Talbot Bay.

The Argyle Diamond Mine in the West Kimberley began operations in 1983 and now produces about six tonnes of gems each year. Most of the output is industrial diamonds, but the five per cent which is gem quality includes the sought-after pink jewels known as "champagne diamonds".

A leafless boab tree in the dry season. The pith of the nuts is eaten by Aborigines.

The mighty Kimberley

The Kimberley was inhabited by Aborigines, and later visited by seafarers from Asia, for a long time before European arrival.

Land in the West Kimberley was taken up by sheep farmers from southwest Western Australia, while the East Kimberley was settled by cattle graziers from Eastern Australia. Gold was discovered at Halls Creek in 1885, but was exhausted by 1887. The Canning Stock Route chain of wells was first used in 1911 to water cattle walking from Halls Creek to the Eastern goldfields.

The idea of irrigating farmland in the Kimberley was put forward by Kimberley Durack in 1937. The Ord River Dam was completed in 1972 and, despite setbacks, irrigation is now producing cattle feed and tropical fruit.

Windjana Gorge, where Jundamurra defied troopers and was killed.

37

Colony without convicts

FACTS

▶ Sturt was accompanied by the experienced bushman Hamilton Hume. They disproved the theory that the rivers west of the Great Dividing Range flowed into an inland sea.

▶ Wakefield wrote *A Letter From Sydney* while serving a three-year sentence for carrying off a 15-year-old heiress, to marry her and gain her money. The marriage was *annulled.

▶ Because of Wakefield's prison term, he was not appointed to the new Board of Commissioners of SA. He refused to have anything to to do with the new colony.

Statue of Colonel Light.

HMS Buffalo brought settlers in 1836.

Tracing the Murray River

In 1828, drought in New South Wales colony resulted in a group led by Captain Charles Sturt setting out to find new pasture inland.

They sailed down the Murrumbidgee River in a whaleboat, then followed the Murray for more than 2500 kilometres to Lake Alexandrina. Then they had to row back against the current.

Make them pay for land

While in prison in England in 1827, Edward Gibbon Wakefield wrote a book outlining his theories for efficiently establishing a new colony:

- There should be no free land grants.
- Land should be sold to settlers who could afford to pay for it.
- The price of land should be high enough to pay for labourers to be brought out from Britain.

Wakefield's idea attracted a group including Robert Gouger, who began a Colonisation Society. The British Government agreed to allow the South Australian Association to begin a new colony on the Gulf of St Vincent. Land was to be sold at 12 *shillings an *acre. There were to be no convicts brought to the colony.

A view of Adelaide and the River Torrens in the late 1800s shows smoke rising from factories.

An aerial view of modern Adelaide and the Torrens, viewed over the northern parklands.

The tree near which the colony was proclaimed.

Lighthouse and historic buildings at Port Adelaide.

The Adelaide Museum, State Library and Art Gallery complex dates back to 1884.

A horse-drawn tram still runs across a causeway from Victor Harbor to Granite Island, SA.

Adelaide on the Torrens

In 1836, settlers landed on Kangaroo Island. Surveyor-General Colonel Light searched for a site for settlement on the mainland before Governor Hindmarsh arrived.

Light drew up excellent plans for Adelaide, but resigned when criticised by the British Government. Hindmarsh and the Resident Commissioner, J.H. Fisher, quarrelled. The settlers, many of them well-educated and with advanced political ideas, were not easy to govern.

George Gawler arrived in 1838 to act as Governor/Resident Commissioner. He spent too freely on roads and buildings, and in 1840 Governor George Grey replaced him. His strict measures saved money, but put many men out of work. Some city unemployed found new jobs in the country and gradually more food became available.

German settlers

German farmers came to South Australia in 1838-39, escaping religious persecution in *Silesia.

Hahndorf was named after Captain Dirk Hahn, who brought 52 families from Silesia in his ship the *Zebra*, then helped them secure land in the Adelaide Hills.

Hahndorf today pays tribute to a pioneer heritage.

39

FACTS

▶ In the 1800s, women were not supposed to run businesses. Mary Penfold's *obituary said "she resided for 48 years at the Grange Vineyards", without mentioning she was the chief winemaker and business head of Penfolds Wines.

▶ In 1840, the European population of SA was about 14 630. The census of 1881 put the population at 276 414.

▶ By 1867, the telegraph linked Adelaide to Melbourne and Sydney. In 1870, the British Australian Telegraph Co. offered to lay a cable from Java to Darwin if the colonies would erect cable from Adelaide to Darwin. The line was completed in 1872.

▶ Iron ore was found at Iron Knob, on the Eyre Peninsula, but lack of coal for smelting delayed development. After 1883, silver-lead from Broken Hill, NSW, was railed to Port Pirie, SA, for *smelting. The ships which took away the lead brought coal as fuel. Port Pirie and Whyalla became industrial towns.

The Barossa Valley, noted for vineyards and wines.

"1844 to evermore"

Mary Penfold and her husband Dr Christopher Penfold emigrated to South Australia in 1844, taking with them vine cuttings from France.

Mary Penfold began making wine at their Magill farm and became a pioneer of Australia's young, vigorous winemaking industry. She introduced new grape varieties, worked to lower State tariff barriers to trade and made the Penfold motto "1844 to evermore" and the Grange Vineyard famous.

Fruits of the vine

By 1860, there were about 8000 German settlers in South Australia.

Those knowledgeable about wine-making discovered that the warm dry summers and cool wet winters of the Barossa Valley and other areas close to Adelaide were ideal for growing grapes. Today, South Australia is known worldwide for its wines.

Picking grapes in South Australia in the late 1800s.

PAA

Wonders of the world

South Australia was rescued from depression with the discovery of rich copper deposits at Kapunda in 1842 and at Burra Burra in 1845. Miners came from Cornwall and Germany to work in these "wonders of the world".

Burra Burra Mine, the "eighth wonder of the world".

PAA

The *Whyalla* was built in Whyalla in 1941 and is now displayed at the Whyalla Maritime Museum.

The railway brought new sights and sounds to the rugged ranges north of Adelaide.

A State with differences

South Australia was different from the other colonies in many ways:

- It never depended on semi-slave convict labour, or on the money which supported convicts.
- It had many small landholders who wanted a share in government, rather than a few squatters who guarded their law-making privileges.
- Labourers were scarce, for many owned land. Labour-saving farming methods and inventions gave a lead to the rest of Australia.
- Many of the early settlers wanted the right to follow their own religious beliefs. They saw education and freedom of speech as important.
- Equal numbers of men and women were present from the earliest days. Women could find ways of life outside traditional female roles.
- Women were given the right to vote in South Australia in 1894. The only other State to achieve this before Federation was Western Australia, in 1899.

Feeding the world

South of Goyder's Line, which links Renmark, Port Augusta and Ceduna, the rainfall and soil of South Australia are suitable for growing crops and for feeding stock.

Farmers who have settled north of this line in rare good seasons have often had to leave their properties when normal dry conditions returned.

Farming worldwide benefited from John Ridley's 1843 invention of a machine to strip the grain from standing wheat. The stump-jump plough, invented by Robert Bowyer Smith on Yorke Peninsula in 1876, turned the soil without jamming or breaking on roots and stumps.

Arid country in the north-west of South Australia.

The Pichi Richi railway runs from Quorn to Woolshed Pass, using historic rolling stock.

41

DID YOU KNOW?

DID YOU KNOW?

FACTS

▶ In 1866, explorer John McKinley recommended Port Darwin as site for a capital. SA Surveyor-General Goyder, whose nickname was "Little Energy", surveyed Darwin rapidly, using Adelaide's grid plan.

▶ Donald Thomson, an *anthropologist, lived with Arnhem Land Aborigines in the 1930s. He described them as "fighting people ... whom I would have liked to lead in action against the Japanese". After World War II, he urged the Federal Government to take responsibility for Aboriginal affairs and land rights.

▶ Uranium was discovered at Rum Jungle, 100 km from Darwin, in 1949, and in 1970 at Nabarlek. Today the Ranger Uranium Mine lies within Kakadu National Park. Mining *royalties are paid to traditional custodians of the land.

▶ Kakadu, in the Top End, and Uluru in central Australia, are National Parks. Their Aboriginal custodians lease these tourist attractions to the Federal Government.

Northern outpost

The British government made three unsuccessful settlements on Australia's northern coast, at Melville Island (1824-28), Raffles Bay (1826-29) and Port Essington (1836-49).

The aim was to control the sea routes to the eastern Indonesian islands and to China, and so to control trade. Poor soil, difficult climate (with monsoon rains and cyclones destroying crops and buildings), the difficulty of obtaining supplies by sea and resistance from the Aborigines all contributed to the abandonment of the three settlements.

Brown's Markets, opened in 1885, shows the solid building style which survived Cyclone Tracy.

Rich pastures were found in the Victoria River district by A.C. Gregory's expedition in 1855. South Australia's pastoralists led the move to take over the Northern Territory in 1863.

After Palmerston (later Darwin) was surveyed in 1869, settlers began arriving in large numbers.

A ship docked at Darwin wharf in the 1880s.

A view of modern Darwin, looking over the Wharf Precinct.

Their land

The Northern Territory is home to many different Aboriginal societies and cultures. Aborigines make up over 22 per cent of the population.

Many Aboriginal groups actively resisted European settlement. Aboriginal labour was vital to the success of cattle stations. In 1972, the Federal Government began a policy of allowing Aboriginal people to decide their own future development. Northern Territory Aborigines have been in the forefront of the land rights movement and have legal title to considerable areas of their traditional lands.

42

WORLD WAR II

No. 23 Squadron Liberators over Darwin, 1945.

During World War II, on 19 February 1942, Darwin was attacked by 93 Japanese bombers with fighter escorts. Shipping was destroyed and 243 people were killed. Sixty-three raids followed. Many people left the city, but the troops remained and Australian and U.S. planes continued to fly from the base.

CYCLONE TRACY

On 25 December, 1974, Cyclone Tracy devastated Darwin. Approximately 36 000 people were evacuated from the flattened city, leaving 11 000 to clean up. A few pre-1974 buildings survive, but today most Darwin buildings are less than 20 years old. They are built to withstand future cyclones.

FACTS

▶ After the first day of raids on Darwin, Japanese Air Force pilots reported they had "used a hammer to crack an egg".

▶ A central Australian town established in 1888 was originally named Stuart after the explorer. It was renamed Alice Springs when the Overland Telegraph station near Alice Springs on the Todd River was transferred to town.

▶ Swamp Buffalo were brought to the NT from Indonesia between 1825 and 1843. Feral buffalos caused damage to wetlands and spread disease and most have now been shot. A number of buffalo are farmed for meat and hides.

At the annual Festival of Darwin Parade today.

Twin Falls, Kakadu National Park, NT.

Alice Springs, in the NT's Red Centre.

Boldly into the unknown

For tens of thousands of years, Aboriginal adventurers travelled the continent of Australia, looking for food, water and new places to live.

These Aborigines were the first of Australia's explorers. By the time Europeans arrived, a network of trade routes covered the continent. Europeans discovered Australia all over again. They were often dependent on Aboriginal guides, who were sometimes far from their own country and people. Without the bushcraft of these Aboriginal companions, and the goodwill of the Aboriginal groups through whose country they passed, far fewer Europeans would have survived their journeys. In 1845, Ludwig Leichhardt noted that his Aboriginal guides remembered the tiniest details about places. He likened their eyes to cameras constantly recording images of the country about them.

Aborigines who accompanied European explorers and often saved their lives included:

Bungaree, who sailed around Australia with Flinders (1801-03) and also sailed with King (1817-18). On his return, he was granted land near Sydney.

Wylie, who trekked across the shores of the Great Australian Bight with his friend Eyre in 1841. His people, at Albany, greeted him with tearful joy, for they had thought him dead.

Yuranigh, who was described by Thomas Mitchell as a "companion, counsellor and friend" on his central Queensland journey in 1846.

Jackey Jackey, who came from Muswellbrook and in 1848 braved Cape York Peninsula with Edmund Kennedy.

Tommy Windich, who repeated Eyre's feat with John Forrest in 1870. In 1874, he travelled from Geraldton to Adelaide. **Tommy Pierre** went on this journey also and in 1879 explored the Kimberley with Alexander Forrest.

Bungaree, of the Broka Bay Aboriginal group, who explored Australia's coasts with Flinders and King.

The sand dune country Eyre and Wylie encountered on their journey from Adelaide to Albany WA.

Members of Forrest's 1874 expedition. Back: Tommy Pierre, Tommy Windich, James Kennedy, James Sweeney. Front: Alexander and John Forrest.

Matthew Flinders sailed around Australia.

Lachlan Macquarie was explorer and Governor.

Charles Sturt traced Murray-Darling system.

Thomas Mitchell explored NSW and Qld.

Who were the explorers?

- Men under orders, such as sailors, soldiers and surveyors.
- Members of expeditions financed by people who hoped they would find pastoral land, minerals, or routes for roads, railways or telegraph lines.
- Glory-hunters, who hoped to earn fame, which could bring fortune.
- Adventurers, who wanted to explore unknown country, set records and gain material for books and films.
- Scientists such as botanists, zoologists and anthropologists, studying plants, animals and cultures.
- Searchers for lost expeditions, or for the legendary inland sea.

Travelling the tough way

Some explorers were killed by Aborigines, or died from thirst, scurvy, other diseases or accident. Survivors of expeditions were often in poor health for years afterwards.

At first, expeditions consisted of physically fit men, who walked or rode horses. Provisions were carried on packhorses or bullock drays. John Horrocks pioneered the use of camels in 1846 (he was killed when one caused his gun to discharge). In the 1900s, motor vehicles, aeroplanes and helicopters and, in Antarctica, Husky dogs and tractors have been used in exploration.

Allan Cunningham found the Darling Downs.

Ludwig Leichhardt went from Qld to NT.

Ernest Giles explored Central Australia.

John McDouall Stuart crossed the continent.

The DIG tree today.

Chambers Pillar was sighted by John McDouall Stuart in 1860.

Where did they go?

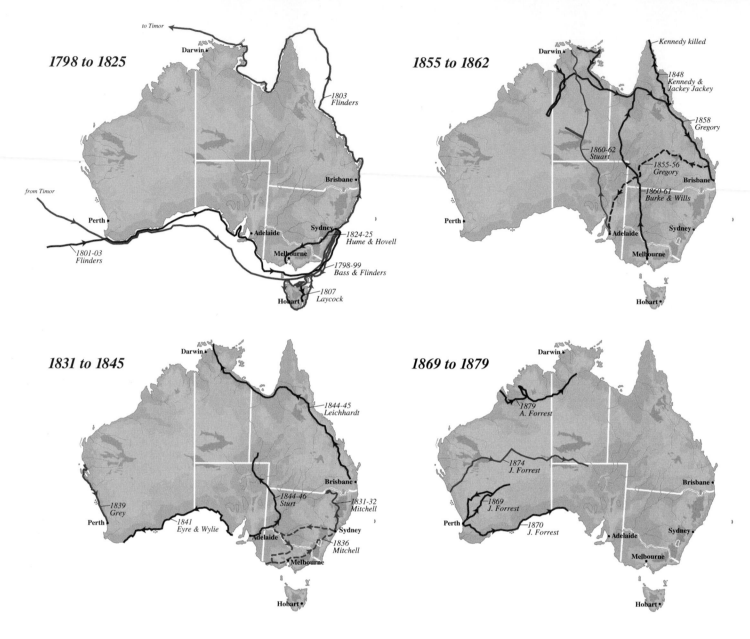

Early explorers had to look after animals, find water, stand watches and cook food, as well as cover long distances and sometimes collect and preserve specimens.

Many scientific instruments, such as *compasses and *barometers, became useless after being jolted in pack-saddles and damaged by dust, sand or damp.

By 1855, Australian-born explorers were seen as the equals of British adventurers.

Successful explorers used bushcraft, were friendly to local Aborigines and carried a minimum of equipment. They sent scouts to locate water ahead of the main party, travelled when it was coolest and looked after their horses or camels well.

The Forrest brothers and the Gregory brothers successfully used survival techniques they had learned from Western Australia's Surveyor-General John Septimus Roe.

A.C. Gregory invented a pack-saddle which relieved pressure on horses' backs and kept them free from sores.

Ludwig Leichhardt took only one set of shoes for each horse for a seven-month trek. At one stage, his horses left blood on the rocks as they walked.

Edward John Eyre could travel at a rate of 40 kilometres per day. Charles Sturt journeyed 3032 kilometres at a rate of 54 kilometres per day.

Expeditions of some of Australia's explorers

1606 Luis de Torres first European to sight Australia. **Willem Jansz** first European to land.

1616 Dirk Hartog names western coast of Australia "Eendrachtsland".

1619 Frederik de Houtman names coastline south of Perth "Dedelsland".

1622 John Brooke first Englishman to see coast. *Tryall* wrecked off WA. *Leeuwin* sights SW of WA.

1627 Pieter Nuyts follows coast from WA to SA. **Francois Thijssen** charts Cape Leeuwin to Nuyts Archipelago, WA.

1629 Francois Pelsaert's *Batavia* wrecked on Houtman Abrolhos. Mutiny and rescue.

1642-43 Abel Tasman discovers Van Diemens Land.

1644 Tasman charts coastline from Gulf of Carpentaria, Qld, to North-West Cape, WA.

1688 William Dampier visits NW coast of WA.

1696-97 Willem de Vlamingh discovers Rottnest Island and Swan R.

1699 Dampier sails coast of NW Australia.

1770 James Cook in *Endeavour* lands at Botany Bay, claims eastern Australia, charts east coast.

1772 St Allouarn claims WA for France.

1788 Arthur Phillip leads settlement at Port Jackson, explores Pitt Water and Hawkesbury R. **Jean de la Perouse** 6 days too late to claim NSW for France. **Henry Lidgbird Ball** finds Lord Howe Is.

1789 William Bligh maps NE coastline of Qld. **Watkin Tench** discovers Nepean R.

1791 George Vancouver discovers King George Sound, WA.

1792-93 Bruni d'Entrecasteaux charts southern coast, Tas. **John Hayes** discovers Risdon Cove, Tas.

1795 George Bass and **Matthew Flinders** sail east coast of NSW in *Tom Thumb*.

1797-98 Bass and **Flinders** find Illawarra Plain, NSW. Bass discovers Western Port, Vic.

1798-99 Bass and **Flinders** circumnavigate Tas.

1801-03 Nicholas Baudin sent by Napoleon Bonaparte to chart New Holland.

1802-03 Flinders circumnavigates Australia.

1803 Charles Grimes discovers Yarra R., Vic. **John Bowen** settles at Risdon Cove, Tas.

1804 David Collins settles at Hobart, Tas.

1807 Thomas Laycock treks across Tas.

1813 Blaxland, Wentworth and **Lawson** find route over Blue Mts, NSW.

1817-18 John Oxley traces Lachlan and Macquarie Rivers, NSW, looking for inland sea.

1817-22 Phillip Parker King charts Qld coastline and Torres Strait.

1818 Louis de Freycinet sent from France.

1821 Throsby and **Wild** find Murrumbidgee R.

1823 John Oxley discovers Brisbane R., Qld.

1824 Hume and **Hovell** sight Australian Alps.

1825 Edmund Lockyer explores Brisbane R., Qld.

1827 James Stirling sails up Swan R., WA. **Allan Cunningham** discovers Darling Downs, Qld.

1828 Cunningham discovers Cunninghams Gap, Qld.

1828-29 Charles Sturt and **Hamilton Hume** travel down Macquarie R., discover Darling R.

1829-30 Charles Sturt follows Murrumbidgee R., names Murray R., discovers it joins Darling R.

1830-34 George Robinson walks around Tas.

1830-36 John Septimus Roe explores WA from Perth to Albany and east to Russell Range.

1831-32 Raphael Clint maps Swan, Canning and Kalgan Rivers, explores Stirling Ranges, WA.

1831-36 Thomas Mitchell discovers Murray-Darling river system.

1832 John Bussell explores Vasse R. area, WA.

1834 Johann Lhotsky explores Australian Alps. **Edward Henty** and family settle Portland Bay, Vic.

1835 John Batman chooses site for Melbourne, Vic.

1836 George Kingston discovers Torrens R., SA.

1837-43 Wickham and **Stokes** in the *Beagle* discover NT rivers and Port Darwin.

1838 James Bremer settles Port Essington, NT.

1838 Edward Eyre overlands stock to SA.

1839 George Grey discovers Gascoyne R., WA.

1840 Paul de Strzelecki explores Gippsland and climbs Mt Kosciusko.

1841 Eyre and **Wylie** cross Nullarbor Plain.

1842 John and **Jane Franklin** discover route from Hobart to Macquarie Harbour, Tas.

1844-45 Ludwig Leichhardt journeys from Brisbane to Port Essington.

1844-45 Charles Sturt survives summer in central Australia.

1845-46 Thomas Mitchell finds Warrego and Barcoo Rivers and opens up central Qld.

1846 A.C. Gregory travels north from Perth, WA.

1846-47 Leichhardt fails to cross continent.

1848 Edmund Kennedy dies on expedition to Cape York Peninsula. **Leichhardt** tries again to travel Qld to WA, but disappears. **A.C. Gregory** finds good land near Geraldton, minerals near Murchison R., WA.

1848-49 John Roe explores from Perth to the Fitzgerald R., WA. **Charles** and **William Archer** pioneer settlement in N Qld.

1855-56 Augustus Gregory and **Ferdinand von Mueller** find good pastures in the NT and Qld.

1859-60 George Dalrymple explores Burdekin R., Qld, and founds town of Bowen.

1860 John McDouall Stuart reaches centre of Australia, finds Macdonnell Ranges.

1860-61 Robert O'Hara Burke and **William Wills** travel from Melbourne to the Gulf of Carpentaria. **FT Gregory** discovers Hamersley Ranges, WA.

1861 Alfred Howitt finds bodies of Burke and Wills, and discovers King living with Aborigines.

1862 Stuart crosses from Adelaide to the Gulf, making Overland Telegraph possible.

1863 John Jardine settles at Somerset, NT.

1864-65 F. and **A. Jardine** and **Richardson** overland cattle up Cape York Peninsula, Qld.

1869 George Goyder surveys site for Darwin, NT.

1870 John Forrest finds route for telegraph line linking WA to the eastern States.

1872 Ernest Giles finds Mount Olga, NT.

1873 William Gosse finds Ayers Rock, NT. **Warburton** crosses continent east to west.

1874 John Forrest travels from WA to central Australia to Adelaide.

1879 Alexander Forrest opens up Kimberley, WA.

1883 Charles Rasp finds silver, lead, zinc at Barrier Range (Broken Hill), NSW.

1893 Patrick Hannan finds gold at Kalgoorlie, WA.

1894 Charles Winnecke leads Horn Scientific Expedition to central Australia.

1895 Bull and **Borchgrevink** land on Antarctica.

1896 Walter Baldwin Spencer and **Francis Gillen** study Aboriginal way of life in central Australia.

1899 Borchgrevink makes first permanent base in Antarctica.

1901 Frederic Drake-Brockman explores centre of Kimberley and finds good grazing land.

1903 Spencer and **Gillen** make final expedition, NW of Lake Eyre.

1906 Alfred Canning surveys stock-route from Wiluna to Halls Creek, WA.

1911-13 Douglas Mawson leads first Australasian Antarctic Expedition.

1923-25 George Wilkins explores Arnhem Land.

1929 Cecil Madigan surveys SA from air.

1929-31 Douglas Mawson leads British, Australian and New Zealand Antarctic Expedition.

1930 Harold Lasseter fails to return from searching for a mythical gold reef in the Petermann Ranges.

1935 Anthropologist Donald Thomson lives with Aborigines in Arnhem Land.

1936 Edward Colson crosses Simpson Desert. **Australian Antarctic Territory** proclaimed.

1940 Charles Mountford investigates Aboriginal culture in the Mann and Musgrave Ranges.

1948 Charles Mountford investigates Aboriginal culture in Arnhem Land.

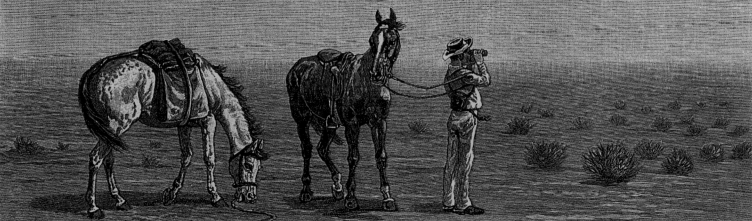

DID YOU KNOW?

FACTS

▶ About 100 species of Australian animals were reported by Europeans before 1788.

▶ Explorers who drew new plants and animals included Mitchell and Sturt. Noted artists who accompanied explorers included Sydney Parkinson (who travelled with Cook), Frederick Bauer (Flinders), Ludwig Becker (Burke and Wills), Thomas Baines (A.C. Gregory) and S.T. Gill (Horrocks).

▶ The English naturalist Charles Darwin visited Australia on the *Beagle* in 1836. The animals he saw contributed to the theories he published 23 years later as *The Origin of the Species by Means of Natural Selection*.

Naturalists in wonderland

The Pied, or Torresian, Imperial-Pigeon, recorded in 1606, was the first truly Australian animal reported by Europeans.

Major Mitchell's Cockatoo, which was first painted by explorer Major Thomas Mitchell.

The Aborigines lived in close physical and spiritual relationships with the animals which lived in their home regions of Australia. They identified the plants which grew in their area and knew each one's usefulness as food, medicine, drug or poison.

Europeans had to discover plants and animals for themselves, although where Aboriginal knowledge was available some naturalists asked for help and advice.

Early expeditions of discovery were often partly financed by scientific groups, and included botanists, zoologists and skilled artists. They collected plants and animals and made pictures of them, the places they saw and the events that happened.

Fine books based on explorers' diaries and sketches of landscapes, Aborigines and wildlife were very popular in the 1800s and those which survive are very valuable.

Joseph Banks, shown in 1773, surrounded by souvenirs of his travels to the South Pacific.

Thomas Baines painted himself and Bowman the horse-keeper meeting Aborigines near the Victoria River, NT, in 1855.

A BOUQUET OF AUSTRALIAN WILDFLOWERS

Sturt's Desert Pea was collected by William Dampier in 1699 on the Dampier Archipelago. It was later named after Charles Sturt who, in 1844-46, explored the Simpson and Sturt's Stony Deserts.

The 75 species of banksia are named after Joseph Banks, "father of Australian botany". Banks took back to England 30 000 plant specimens, nearly one-third Australian and new to science.

Botanist Robert Brown and artist Ferdinand Bauer accompanied Matthew Flinders on *Investigator*. The plants they collected included grevilleas, which supplied the Aborigines with sweet nectar.

Georgiana Molloy collected seed of Western Australian plants such as Mangles' Kangaroo Paw (above) for English and German botanists. A scented boronia is named after her.

A waratah like the one shown here was painted in watercolours in 1788-90 by Captain John Hunter, later Governor of NSW. Before photography, army and navy officers needed to be able to sketch.

William Dampier collected a coastal wattle at Shark Bay, WA. A wattle from Van Diemen's land was being grown in England in 1780 from seed collected in 1777, on Cook's third voyage.

FACTS

▶ Botany Bay was named Stingrays Bay by Cook. The name was changed because of the great number of plants there.

▶ When Joseph Banks returned to London from his voyage with Cook in the *Endeavour*, he set five artists to add to the 1000 sketches of plants made by Sydney Parkinson before he died in Djakarta in 1771. The *Florilegium*, containing 738 colour plates of these plants, was not published until the 1980s.

▶ Cook made two more voyages to the South Seas. In 1777, at Adventure Bay, Tasmania, David Nelson and surgeon-botanist William Anderson collected plants and seeds.

▶ William Gosse, who travelled from Alice Springs to Perth in 1873, said eating quandong fruit kept his men in good health.

FACTS

▶ De Vlamingh was the first European to write of a wallaby's pouch. He described the "bag or purse ... into which one could put one's hand" of the female Quokka.

▶ In 1808, the person caring for a Common Wombat brought back by Flinders from a Bass Strait island wrote: "It allowed children to pull and carry it about, and when it bit them did not appear to do it in anger or with violence".

▶ Wedge-tailed Eagles were seen by William Dampier in 1699.

▶ Cook recorded the shooting of an Australian Bustard. Banks wrote that it was "the best we have eat since we left England". The first Australian bird to reach England alive was a Rainbow Lorikeet, taken aboard *Endeavour* as a pet.

▶ Arthur Phillip described a goanna or monitor lizard in 1789. He also wrote of the Port Jackson Shark, and of a Wobbegong Shark which lay on a ship's deck for 2 hours, then seized a passing dog by the leg.

SOME EARLY RECORDS OF AUSTRALIAN ANIMALS

Volckertzoon (1656) and de Vlamingh (1696) recorded Quokkas on Rottnest Is., WA.

In 1792 Hunter wrote that the wombat has a "false belly for the security of its young".

In 1798, John Price noted that Aborigines at Bargo, NSW, called this animal "a cullawine".

In 1792, William Bligh sketched a Short-beaked Echidna and noted its snout and that its mouth "opens at the extremity and will not admit anything above the size of a pistol ball".

A Platypus was captured in the Hawkesbury River, NSW, by David Collins in 1797. This Platypus was painted by John Lewin, who landed in 1800 and published the first book on Australian birds.

A Rainbow Lorikeet survived Cook's first voyage. It was painted in England in 1774.

Allan Cunningham saw a Frilled Lizard perched on a tree stump at Port Nelson, WA, in 1820.

Arthur Phillip described a "beautiful lizard" with a forked tongue. This is Gould's Monitor.

At Endeavour River, Qld, in 1770, Cook recorded crew members had shot an animal which "jumped like a Hare or a dear". The Eastern Grey Kangaroo proved to be good to eat.

De Vlamingh saw Emu tracks in 1697. An Emu was sighted when the First Fleet arrived and one was shot near Sydney Cove soon after. In 1793, naval officer Watkin Tench recorded a nest of 12 eggs.

Splendour in books

Aborigines have illustrated Australia's animals for at least 50 000 years. The last 200 years have seen the publication of some magnificent natural history books.

John Lewin arrived in Sydney in 1800 on the *Mercury*. In 1808, he published *The Birds of New Holland*, the first book on Australian birds.

In 1838, John and Elizabeth Gould came to Australia. John observed and collected birds and mammals while Elizabeth illustrated them. After she died in 1841, Gould engaged other artists and in 1848 published *The Birds of Australia*. Between 1845 and 1863 Gould produced another great work, *The Mammals of Australia*.

This hand-coloured lithograph of Red-tailed Black-Cockatoos was published in Gould's *The Birds of Australia*.

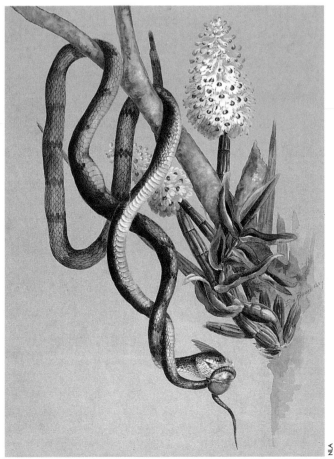

Ellis Rowan painted this watercolour of a Brown Tree-snake with a Waxbill Finch near a tree orchid in 1887.

Women and the wilds

Women who advanced natural history in Australia in the 1800s were often botanists or botanical artists.

They included Tasmania's Jane, Lady Franklin, and Louisa Anne Meredith, and New South Wales's Caroline Louisa Atkinson and Fanny Macleay. Ellis Rowan was a noted botanical artist who worked in the wilds of Northern Queensland. Harriet and Helena Scott ably illustrated books on the snakes and insects of Australia.

Amalie Dietrich was a professional collector, who laboured tirelessly in Australia for the Hamburg Museum of Natural History from 1863 to 1872.

FACTS

▶ John Gilbert collected birds, mammals and insects from many parts of Australia for Gould. He joined Ludwig Leichhardt's expedition to the NT and in 1845 was speared to death near the Gulf of Carpentaria. A memorial tablet, at St James's Church, Sydney, reads: *How sweet and fitting it is to die for science.*

▶ Gould's books were illustrated with lithographs. A drawing made on fine-grained sandstone was transferred to paper then hand-coloured.

▶ Nests, eggs and stuffed birds were being photographed long before 1889, when A.J. Campbell took the first Australian picture of living birds, Crested Terns on Rottnest Is., WA.

▶ After 1903, Australia's A.H.E. Mattingley photographed baby egrets dying after their parents had been killed to provide feathers for women's hats. These pictures ended the Australian plume trade.

Treasures from the earth

Gold-rushes brought immigrants to New South Wales and Victoria in the 1850s, to Queensland in the 1870s, to the Northern Territory in the 1880s and to Western Australia in the 1890s. The increase in population and wealth led to many changes in Australia.

During the late 1800s, minerals such as coal, iron and tin became the basis for industrial development. As the 1900s progressed, new technology brought increased demand for minerals such as nickel, bauxite, uranium, oil and natural gas. Mining created new communities, often in remote areas.

Gold-discoverer Hargraves (and his horse) shown returning the salutes of gold miners.

S.T. Gill showed an entire family hard at work on the Bendigo goldfields on 1 July 1852.

Mining opal by hand.

After 1870, machine drills allowed mining deep underground.

Early industrial action

Silver was found by Paddy Green in western New South Wales in 1875. Charles Rasp, a boundary rider, found silver, lead and zinc ores near today's Broken Hill in 1883.

In 1885, Broken Hill Proprietary Limited (BHP) began operations. Broken Hill became one of the world's great mining centres. In 1892, the failure of a miners' strike over pay, and of strikes in other industries, made working people realise that they must get their representatives into parliament.

Broken Hill Trades Hall was built in 1905.

An aerial view of a Hamersley iron mine shows the terraces caused by open cut mining at bottom left.

Country of red iron

In 1889, Western Australian Government *Geologist Woodward reported that in the Pilbara "iron occurs in immense lodes … there is enough to supply the whole world" but that the area was too remote for development.

In the 1930s, in the lead-up to World War II, the Australian Government stopped Australian iron ore exports, partly to avoid supplying Japan's steel industry. In the 1950s the export bans were lifted and the vast iron ore deposits of north-western Australia were opened up.

Australia has large coal resources.

Salt is an important mineral product.

FACTS

▶ Lang Hancock, grazier and amateur geologist, was flying through a deep Hamersley gorge when he saw rain streaming down sheer 60-metre walls of a substance he thought was pure iron.

▶ Mount Isa, in western Qld, is the site of Australia's largest underground mine. Silver, lead, zinc and copper come from "the Isa".

▶ Today, Australia is a leading producer of coal, diamonds, aluminium, iron, nickel, gold, copper and zinc. Australia produces 95% of the world's opals, as well as sapphires and pearls.

▶ Today, Hamersley ore is taken by trains, each over two kilometres in length, to the port of Dampier, to be exported in huge bulk carriers.

▶ Since living things cannot exist without water, it could be termed Australia's most valuable mineral.

Feeding the people

Irrigation allows intensive planting of a variety of crops.

The real Aussie battlers

While squatters "sat down" on large areas of land, and could become rich, selectors arrived 20 to 30 years later and bought smaller pieces of land.

Some selectors had been gold diggers. Some were immigrants. They seldom had much money and often the father of a family worked on a squatter's run, in a sawmill or at another job, while mother and children kept the farm going. A settler could be deeply in debt to a bank. Squatter and selector could clash over straying stock, water rights, weed-control or fences.

Machines have replaced human labour on many farms.

Governor Phillip set aside land at Farm Cove for farming. This land is now the Royal Botanic Gardens.

He quickly realised free settlers with farming experience were needed and by the time he left in 1792 had established 68 farmers on small holdings at Parramatta and other places. Crops grown included wheat, barley, flax, maize and oats.

A glamorised advertising picture of women's work on a farm one hundred years ago.

Troubles and hardships

The Australian farmer has to deal with some or all of the following: soil which is poor in plant foods; drought; flood; erosion; increasingly salty water and soil; plagues of rabbits, mice and locusts; and introduced weeds.

Attempts to poison pests and fertilise land can result in further problems, such as polluted rivers.

Golden grain

New machinery such as the stump-jump plough, new ways of clearing mallee land and the use of *superphosphate expanded the wheat industry in the 1890s.

Railway networks developed through wheat-growing areas. In 1901, William Farrer's experiments with wheat-breeding resulted in "Federation", an early-maturing, high-yielding strain.

Regular, predictable rainfall and suitable soil are necessary for successful cereal crop farming.

Wheat-farming in SA in the late 1800s.

Government controls

In 1915, during World War I, the Federal Government took control of all wheat grown in Australia.

This meant guaranteed prices for farmers. It also opened the way for governments to support farmers by placing duties on imported farm products of all sorts, and paying *subsidies to help farmers grow crops.

Other nations such as the European Common Market and the USA now sell their surplus food so cheaply that Australian farmers find it hard to compete. In the late 1900s, many small farmers have been forced to leave the land, and see their farms become part of large company holdings.

What is a living wage?

In 1882, 17-year-old Hugh McKay, who disliked the heavy labour of separating grain from chaff, invented a *combine harvester and made the *prototype from bits of farm machinery. It took years to perfect. Eventually, McKay built a manufacturing empire.

In the early 1900s, a dispute between McKay and the union representing the workers in his Sunshine Harvesters factory was taken to court. In 1907, the new Federal Arbitration Commission handed down the Harvester Judgement. This set a minimum, or basic, wage for an unskilled working man of seven shillings per day (McKay was paying six).

Tropical fruits are popular crops in northern Australia.

Flocks, herds and mobs

Early settlers pushed into new territory to find grazing land for sheep and cattle. In the 1800s, the textile mills of Britain bought colonial wool and by 1849 there were almost 16 million sheep in Australia. The first shipment of frozen meat left Sydney in 1879.

Cattle, sheep, pigs and poultry are still the main animals farmed. Wool was Australia's major rural export until the mid-1970s, but meat has become increasingly important. Today many farms produce both livestock and grain or other crops.

Shearers using machine-driven shears.

In time of drought, sheep graze slowly along the "long paddock" of the roadside reserves.

Wool barge being towed by paddle-steamer along the Darling River in the 1870s.

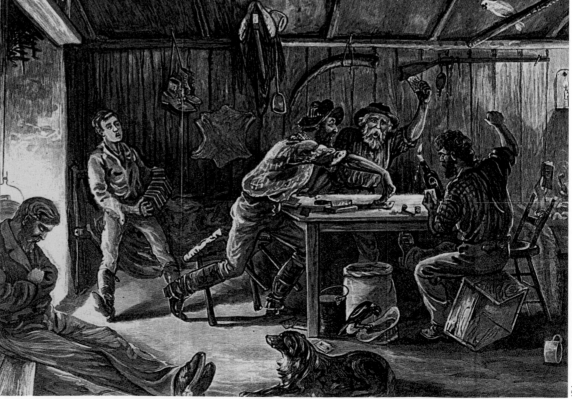

"In the men's hut" shows stockmen of the late 1800s enjoying themselves after a hard day's work.

The drover's best mates were his dog and his horses. This photograph was taken between 1900 and 1910.

Children on a station in outback Queensland in 1917. They would have ridden to school or been educated at home.

Today's grazier may work the property alone because of the high cost of labour.

THE LABOR PARTY WAS BORN UNDER A TREE

From the 1870s, labourers joined unions, which were prepared to strike unless they were given better conditions and wages. In a time of depression in 1891, Queensland shearers formed a union and went on strike against terrible working conditions and low wages. Graziers brought in workers from New Zealand and locked union members out of their properties. Urged on by the graziers, the State government sent in police and soldiers. After violence erupted and 13 shearers were gaoled, a meeting of the Australian Workers' Union under a gum tree at Barcaldine gave birth to the Labor Party. On 1 December 1899, the world's first Labor Government sat in Brisbane.

DID YOU KNOW?

FACTS

▶ A Huon Pine felled in Tasmania's south-west in the 1970s proved to be approximately 2500 years old.

▶ Each year from 1788 to 1980 approximately 500 000 ha of Australia was cleared of trees. In 1847, it was said that the Big Scrub in northern NSW could not be cleared within 500 years. By 1900, it was gone.

▶ Since hardwood trees may take 60 years to grow big enough for logging, it is not economic to cultivate them and they are taken from native forests. Softwood pine plantations can be logged within 30 years.

▶ The National Association of Forest Industries notes that nationwide about 85 000 people are employed in growing and processing wood. Wood processing employs 20% of Tasmania's workforce.

▶ Australia has 20 000 sq km of rainforests, containing the greatest concentration of ancient lifeforms found anywhere on Earth. 40% is outside conservation reserves.

Timber!

Until 20 million years ago, most of Australia was covered by subtropical or tropical rainforest.

As the continent cooled and dried, rainforest areas shrank and stands of eucalypts and acacias took their place. Mammals such as the Koala and possums, birds such as honeyeaters and many types of insects developed with these plants.

Before Europeans arrived, less than 10% of Australia was forested. The best growth was on good soils in higher rainfall areas, in places which were desirable for agriculture. Wasteful clearing and logging of forests are part of modern Australian history. The importance of preserving old forests and regenerating logged areas is now acknowledged.

Hardwood timber, sawn and ready for use.

Leadbeater's Possum, seen here licking sap, is one of the rarest of the animals which need old forests containing hollow trees for their survival.

Australia's temperate rainforests have been logged for fine timbers.

Giants of the past

The world's largest flowering plant is Australia's Mountain Ash, which grows in limited locations in mountainous regions of Tasmania and Victoria.

A Mountain Ash felled at Watts River, Victoria, in 1872 was probably 150 metres tall (higher than the arch of Sydney Harbour bridge). A tree 122 metres tall had a trunk 22 metres around. The modern record for this tree is 95 metres.

Trees cleared from agricultural land have traditionally been ringbarked, left to die and then burned.

Pastoralists used whatever timber was on their properties to build stockyards and fences.

Regrowth Karri forest, in SW WA, has many years to go before equalling the giant trees of bygone times.

Almost all the money available to forest management bodies comes from sales of wood.

The Daintree rainforest in north Queensland was once logged for Red Cedar and other fine timber. It was World Heritage-listed in 1988.

Sweet scents

By 1850, sandalwood provided nearly half of WA's export income.

Fragrant oil is distilled from this small tree, and it still earns WA about 10 million dollars annually.

Old forests

Old forests contain mature, hollow-limbed trees, and have been little disturbed by logging or burning.

They are necessary for the survival of rare animals, including Leadbeater's Possum, many other possums and gliders, cockatoos and owls.

The Mountain Ash forest of Gippsland, a living cathedral and a sanctuary for rare wildlife.

St Patrick's Cathedral, Melbourne, *consecrated in 1897. The pews show a traditional use of fine timber.

Looking after land and sea

▶ There are 2.2 humans per square kilometre of land in Australia, but much of the continent is desert.

▶ For 200 years, "developing" land has meant clearing it, sowing foreign crops and replacing soft-footed native animals with hard-hooved sheep and cattle. Introduced European animals and plants have often run wild. Some, like foxes and cats, kill native species.

▶ The droughts and floods which characterise Australia's weather are produced by the El Nino Southern Oscillation (ENSO). Changes in ocean currents along the west coast of South America result in the ocean around Australia becoming colder. Fewer clouds form, less rain falls over the continent and drought results. When ENSO changes again, and the seas become warmer around Australia, flooding rains may result.

▶ The 1981 Whale Protection Act protects whales within 320 km of the Australian coast.

Australia is the world's second-driest continent, where most rain evaporates before it enters the soil. Humans have altered the natural landscapes, and introduced foreign animals and plants.

Environmental problems faced today include increased salinity of soil and water, loss of topsoils, water and air pollution, loss of *ozone from the air and extinction of some animals and plants.

One hope for the future is for farmers, graziers and scientists to work together. They could focus on making farming land productive over a long time, instead of looking for record yields for a few years. Replacement of some of the cleared vegetation would reduce *erosion and rising salt levels.

Today it is accepted that some areas of land should be regarded as national heritage and kept as close as possible to their original state. Places which attract large numbers of tourists, such as coral reefs, rainforests and desert need to be managed with special care, so they are not "loved to death".

Sand dune plants in one of Australia's vast inland deserts flower briefly after a rare, heavy fall of rain.

This bare landscape once carried thick forest, but was devastated by logging and mining wastes.

The seas around us

In 1995, the United Nations granted Australia rights over the area extending 200 nautical miles from its coastline.

Australia now oversees an area of water more than one-and-a-half times its land area. The resources of sea and sea-bed include marine life, minerals and natural gas. Over-fishing and wasteful fishing, destruction of estuaries and mangrove "fish nurseries" and pollution of coastal waters are continuing problems.

Humpback Whales are increasing in numbers.

ENDANGERED SPECIES

The Northern Hairy-nosed Wombat is endangered.

The threatened Southern Cassowary.

*In the past 200 years, 17 species of Australian mammal and three species of bird have disappeared. Nine mammal species survive only on offshore islands. *Habitat destruction, disease, introduced predators and competitors and human hunting are to blame. Captive breeding and release in suitable areas which are then kept clear of predators may save some rare species. Among the most threatened mammals and birds are the Southern Right Whale, Humpback Whale, Dugong, Hairy-nosed Wombat, Rufous Hare-wallaby, Bridled Nailtail Wallaby, Noisy Scrub-bird, Helmeted Honeyeater, Southern Cassowary and a number of parrots and cockatoos.*

FACTS

▶ If a place is chosen for World Heritage listing, the nation responsible for it undertakes that it will protect, conserve and pass it down to future generations. Australia's Federal Government can act to protect a World Heritage area, as it did the Franklin River in 1983 and Queensland's Wet Tropics in 1987.

PRESERVED, PROTECTED AND PASSED DOWN

AUSTRALIA'S WORLD HERITAGE AREAS

East Coast Temperate and Sub-Tropical Rainforest Parks, NSW and Qld
•
Great Barrier Reef, Qld
•
Great Sandy Region, Qld
•
Kakadu National Park, NT
•
Lord Howe Island Group
•
Tasmanian Wilderness
•
Uluṟu-Kata Tjuṯa National Park, NT
•
Wet Tropics Region, Qld
•
Willandra Lakes Region, NSW
•
Shark Bay, WA
•
Riversleigh, Qld
•
Naracoorte, SA

Many areas of Australia are listed as national parks, historic sites, nature or scientific reserves. Set up and managed by the States and Territories, they vary in size and importance from many square kilometres to tiny places next to roads or waterways. The Commonwealth manages Kakadu and Uluṟu-Kata Tjuṯa National Parks in association with the traditional Aboriginal owners. Also, Australia takes responsibility for protecting a number of Biosphere Reserves, which contain examples of particular habitats.

These reserves include:
Uluṟu-Kata Tjuṯa National Park, NT
Kosciusko National Park, NSW
the Prince Regent River Reserve, WA
Southwest National Park, Tas
Fitzgerald River National Park, WA
Wilsons Promontory National Park, Vic
Macquarie Island Nature Reserve, NSW
Croajingolong National Park, Vic
Hattah/Murray-Kulkyne National Park, Vic
Yathong National Park, NSW
Bookmark National Park, SA

Kakadu National Park, NT.

The Willandra Lakes Region, NSW.

Colonies to States to Commonwealth

From 1788 to 1850, Britain had the final say on laws made to govern the colonies. However, as time went by each colony gained more power over the way it was run.

By 1828, New South Wales had a Legislative Council of 10 to 15 men. A majority vote could prevent the Governor passing a law. In 1842, the power and size of the Council were increased. Two-thirds of its members were to be elected by men who owned property. The Australian Colonies Government Act of 1850 separated Port Phillip from New South Wales. It set up Legislative Councils in Victoria, Tasmania, South Australia and Western Australia.

In the second half of the 1800s, although Australians were allowed to make laws about many subjects Britain still decided important issues. Increasingly the colonies felt that they, and not the British Government, should deal with problems concerning trade, foreign policy and defence.

Sir Henry Parkes, a far-sighted politician.

Makers and shakers

William Charles Wentworth was born in Sydney in 1790.

He explored the Blue Mountains in 1813. After becoming a lawyer in England, he took up large holdings of land in New South Wales and was deeply involved in the political reforms of 1842 and 1850.

Henry Parkes arrived in Sydney from England in 1839. He became a leading figure in New South Wales politics and worked for the federation of the States into the Commonwealth of Australia, chairing the 1891 Federal Convention.

Vida Goldstein was born in Victoria in 1869. She fought for women's rights in the workplace and their right to vote. She founded many organisations to aid women and was one of the first women in the British Empire to stand for election to a parliament.

This painting by Tom Roberts depicts the opening of the first Commonwealth Parliament on 9 May 1901.

A nation is born

Seven representatives from each colony met in 1891 to draw up a *constitution for governing Australia.

It was decided that the new Federal Parliament was to consist of a House of Representatives and a Senate. The States were to make laws on most matters, while Federal Government controlled customs duties, defence and the armed forces. Where State and Federal laws came into conflict, the Federal Supreme Court was to make the final ruling.

After fierce debate, especially in Western Australia and Queensland, the States agreed. The Commonwealth of Australia finally came into being on 1 January 1901.

Federal Parliament sat in the Victorian Houses of Parliament, Melbourne, from 1901 to 1927.

The opening of the present Parliament House by Queen Elizabeth II in 1988.

63

Australia's capital

FACTS

▶ Throsby Smith, Wild and Vaughn rode onto the Limestone Plains in 1820. The area where Canberra now stands was the home of about 500 Aborigines, mainly of the Walgalu and Ngunawal groups.

▶ The name Canberra comes from the Aboriginal word "camberry", meaning a meeting place.

▶ In 1825, a Sydney merchant, Robert Campbell, was granted a grazing property he named Duntroon.

▶ Convicts worked on properties in the Canberra district until 1840.

▶ Fierce rivalry existed between Sydney and Melbourne. Canberra, more or less midway between the battling capitals, was acceptable to both.

▶ For reasons of defence, the Federal Capital was sited inland. Canberra has access to the sea at Jervis Bay.

▶ The foundation stone marking the city of Canberra was laid on 12 March 1913.

A view of Canberra, looking across Parliament House to Lake Burley Griffin and Mount Ainslie.

Blundell's Farmhouse was built in 1860 for William Ginn, the Campbell family's ploughman. The next tenant, George Blundell, had eight children.

Duntroon House, which belonged to the Campbells for 70 years, is now the Officers' Mess of a military college.

A meeting place

Places suggested as the site of Australia's federal government, included Melbourne, Sydney, Tumut and Alice Springs.

Parliament sat in Melbourne while many sites were inspected. In 1901, Tasmanian politician King O'Malley proposed that an area of not less than 1000 square miles of land should be secured in a fertile situation. Yass-Canberra, on the limestone flats of the Molonglo River, was chosen.

The Federal Labor government of Andrew Fisher organised a worldwide design competition for the new city. It was won by Chicago landscape architect Walter Burley Griffin, who did his best to oversee construction until 1920, when he left Canberra. His grand design for the city was finally realised by the flooding of Lake Burley Griffin in 1964 and by a new Parliament House in 1988.

A provisional building

Canberra's first Parliament House was intended to serve until a grander building could be erected.

Burley Griffin was horrified that it was to be placed in front of his site for a permanent Parliament House on Capital Hill. He said it would be "like filling the front yard with outhouses". In 1927, the building was opened with a gold key by the Duke of York (later King George VI). Dame Nellie Melba sang "God Save the King", the national anthem of the day. Tragically, after the official fly-past, a plane crashed, killing the pilot.

No cost was spared

Canberra's present Parliament House occupies most of Capital Hill.

The complex, which has 4500 rooms, took eight years to build and cost over one billion dollars. The main structural features are two massive granite walls, shaped like back-to-back boomerangs. The stainless steel flagpole is 81 metres high, the mosaic in the forecourt contains over 100 000 pieces of granite. In the complex are more than 3000 artworks and documents, including the original Act of Constitution of Australia, as well as one of the four copies of the 1297 Magna Carta.

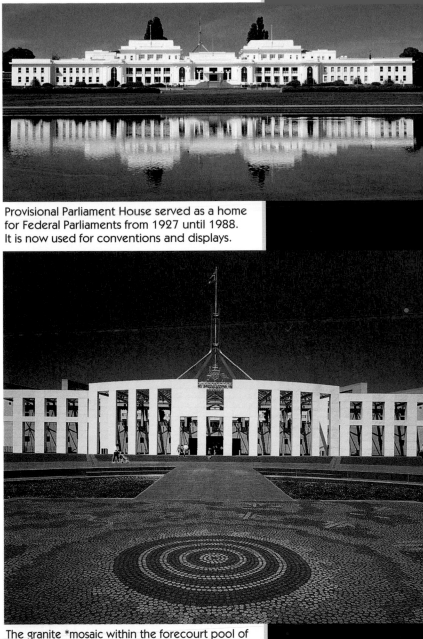

Provisional Parliament House served as a home for Federal Parliaments from 1927 until 1988. It is now used for conventions and displays.

The granite *mosaic within the forecourt pool of Parliament House was designed by Michael Tjakamarra Nelson and represents a meeting place.

The High Court of Australia rules on matters affecting the Constitution. This building was opened in 1980.

The Anglican Church of St John the Baptist in Reid was consecrated in 1845.

65

In time of war

▶ Until the 1850s, an Aborigine could launch 10 spears, accurate over 100 m, while a White was reloading after firing two shots.

▶ Pemulwuy led the Eora people against the colonists from 1790 until 1802.

▶ The "rising sun" badge on the Australian digger's hat represents an arc of bayonets.

▶ Ballarat, Vic, has the longest war memorial in the world, a 22-km row of trees, each honouring a soldier.

Aboriginal resistance

The British Government did not acknowledge Aboriginal title to land, or that a state of war could exist with Aborigines. Civilians and police crushed Aboriginal resistance to White settlement.

Most Aborigines preferred to use spears rather than guns when fighting, and they were most successful using *guerilla tactics rather than direct battle. After the 1850s, quick-loading firearms gave the Whites the advantage, and the use of Aboriginal (native) police, in areas remote from their own country, proved decisive. It is estimated that between 1788 and the 1930s at least 20 000 Aborigines and over 2000 non-Aboriginal people were killed in this conflict.

Memorial to Boer War dead, Adelaide.

Veterans at an Anzac Day ceremony.

Diorama at the Australian War Memorial, Canberra, shows troops advancing.

The Australian War Memorial on Anzac Avenue, Canberra.

The terrible toll of 1914-'18

While Australia was part of the British Empire, colonial troops supported Britain in time of war.

Australians fought at Khartoum in North Africa (1885) and in the Boer War in South Africa (1889-1902). When Britain declared war on Germany in August 1914, Australia did so as well.

Around 60 000 Australians, out of a population of five million, died in World War I. In many communities, every second man between the ages of 18 and 45 enlisted. One in five did not return. The heroic but unsuccessful assault by Australian and New Zealand troops on strong Turkish fortifications on the Gallipoli Peninsula in 1915 resulted in the deaths of 8141 Australians. After Gallipoli, Australian troops fought in France and the Middle East. Feeling against the war slowly grew in Australia, and in referendums in 1916 and 1917 the people rejected *conscription to boost troop numbers. The war ended in 1918.

By 1919, the tradition of the tough Aussie soldier had been born. Anzac Day, 25 April, became a day of national remembrance for the fallen in all wars.

WORLD WAR II

Germany invaded Poland on 1 September 1939. Britain and Australia then declared war on Germany. Australian troops fought against Germans and their Italian allies, mainly in North Africa, the Middle East and the Mediterranean Sea.

Japan invaded South-East Asia to gain an empire which would supply oil, tin and rubber, and other raw materials. After the attack on the United States naval base at Pearl Harbour, Hawaii, on 7 December 1941, the United States of America and Australia declared war.

Australians quickly realised that Britain could not defend them in this threatening situation. Prime Minister John Curtin defied the British Government and brought Australian troops back to fight for their country. The 1942 Battle of the Coral Sea and

An Australian soldier wounded on the Kokoda Trail in New Guinea is carried from a plane in Port Moresby in 1942.

the New Guinea campaign of 1942-44 were two decisive actions in a conflict which made Australia look to the USA rather than Britain for support.

The war ended in 1945, after nearly 40 000 Australians, out of a population of seven million, had been killed and the Anzac legend had been reinforced. Many women had entered the workforce, often in new occupations. The Federal Government had gained new powers, some of which it was to retain.

FACTS

▶ 96 Australians have been awarded the Victoria Cross, the highest British award for bravery in battle. The Australian Victoria Cross was introduced in 1991. So far, none has been awarded.

▶ Australians fought in Korea between 1950 and 1953, as part of a United Nations Command. Losses totalled 339.

▶ 17 424 conscripts actually served in Vietnam. They were chosen by ballot, which was quickly nicknamed "the lottery of death".

Conflict over Vietnam

In 1962, Australia followed the United States of America in supporting the government of South Vietnam against the communist-backed government of the country's north.

At first few Australians objected to military involvement in Vietnam. After conscription was introduced in 1964, to meet commitments to send troops to a number of South-East Asian countries, this attitude changed. By 1971, public demonstrations showed clearly that many Australians wanted to end involvement in Vietnam. About 50 000 Australians served there between 1962 and 1973. Two hundred and thirty-five regular troops and 202 conscripts died in Vietnam.

The way in which anti-war protests were made, including the use of demonstrations, was to provide a model for the activities of supporters of the women's, Aboriginal and environmental movements of the 1970s and 1980s.

National Soldiers Memorial, Adelaide.

Talents of body and mind

Painting Australia's light

The first Australian artists were Aborigines, and today the value of work produced by indigenous artists is recognised worldwide.

The first oil painting produced in Australia was a view of Sydney Cove completed in 1794 by the convict Thomas Watling. Artists of the early 1800s included John Glover, Mary Morton Allport, Georgiana McCrae, Conrad Martens and, later, Eugene von Guerard, Louis Buvelot and William Strutt.

In the late 1800s, the Heidelberg School, whose main figures were Arthur Streeton, Tom Roberts, Frederick McCubbin and Charles Condor, painted the Australian landscape in new ways.

The Wynne Prize for landscape painting was first awarded in 1897. The founder of *The Bulletin*, J.F. Archibald, also inaugurated the Archibald Prize, awarded for the best portrait of a distinguished person.

A miniature self-portrait on ivory by pioneer, artist and writer Georgiana McCrae (1804-1890).

La Trobe Picture Collection, State Library of Victoria

Books and writers

The first book published in Australia, in 1802, was a collection of government orders. John Lewin's *Birds of New South Wales* (1813) was the first illustrated book.

The first Australian novel, published in 1830, was *Quintus Servinton* by ex-convict Henry Savery. In 1823, the explorer William Charles Wentworth was the first Australian-born author to have his work published. Banjo Paterson was the most famous of the bush poets of the late 1800s and early 1900s. Henry Lawson was a noted short-story writer and novelist, Ethel Robertson (Henry Handel Richardson) was a well-known novelist and C.J. Dennis was a poet of the city streets.

Tom Roberts, Bailed Up, 1895–1927, oil on canvas, 134.5 x 182.8 cm, The Art Gallery of New South Wales.

Heard and seen

The first direct overseas radio message reached Australia from England in 1918. Australia's first radio station, Sydney's 2BL, went to air in 1923. The oldest surviving commercial radio station is Sydney's 2UE.

Australia's first telecast was made by Bruce Gyngell on Channel TCN-9, Sydney, in 1956.

On the set of "The Romance of Runnibede", 1907.

Nellie Melba, soprano, toast of the operatic world.

Operatic stars

Nellie Melba (Helen Porter Mitchell) changed her name to honour her home city, Melbourne. She ruled the opera stage from 1892 to 1926.

Considering Dame Nellie's successors, including Dame Joan Sutherland, one overseas critic remarked, "Australia produces great singers the way it does sheep!"

Images on a big screen

The first Australian film, *Soldiers of the Cross*, was made in 1900 by the Salvation Army. "Salvo" members played Christian martyrs in a tennis court disguised as a Roman arena, and in front of the lions' cage at Fitzgerald's Circus.

The Story of the Kelly Gang was made in 1906. Since then, Australian film classics have included *Forty Thousand Horsemen* (1940), *Picnic at Hanging Rock* (1975), *Gallipoli* (1981), *Crocodile Dundee* (1986), *Strictly Ballroom* (1992) and *Shine* (1996).

Melbourne's Princess Theatre opened in 1886 with *The Mikado* starring the popular Nelly Stewart.

FACTS

▶ Waltzing Matilda was written by Banjo Paterson and put to music by Christina McPherson, on Dagworth Station, Qld, in 1895. It was published in 1903.

▶ In the 1930s, test cricket action was cabled to Australia. Sportscasters recreated the action on air, tapping a pencil on a piece of wood to imitate bat hitting ball.

▶ Felix the Cat, a comic and film cartoon character, was created 10 years before Mickey Mouse, in 1919, by Pat Sullivan of Sydney.

▶ The Australian Broadcasting Commission was born on 1 July 1932. Until 1941, evening announcers wore evening dress.

▶ *Blue Hills*, a popular rural soapie, ran on ABC radio for 5795 episodes from 1949 to 1976.

▶ The Logies for TV achievement were named after John Logie Baird, Scots TV pioneer.

A passion for action

The Australian passion for sport is famous. Many Australians are active players, while many more are enthusiastic spectators.

Two hundred years ago, hunting, fishing, horse-racing and boxing were popular sports. After 1850, improved transport, the use of electric light, the invention of rubber tyres and the use of sewing machines for uniforms boosted team and individual sports. The telegraph allowed sporting results to be received quickly. In the 1900s, radio, and later television, transformed sport into both mass entertainment and big business.

The first cricket team to represent Australia abroad, in 1868, was made up of Aborigines. They ended their England tour with 14 wins, 14 losses and 19 draws. The draws were usually due to rain.

A modern Melbourne Cup.

A dinkum Aussie game

In Melbourne in 1858, Thomas Wills and his cousin combined features of rugby, soccer and *hurling into a game called Australian Rules football.

At first goalposts were 1.6 kilometres apart and each team had 40 players. The rules were drawn up in 1866, and an oval-shaped ball was first used in 1867.

Carbine wins the 1890 Melbourne Cup.

Australian Rules football being played on an oddly-shaped Melbourne football ground in 1883.

THE ALL-CONQUERING DON

Don Bradman's cricket career was interrupted by World War II. Over 20 years, at a time when far fewer matches were played each season than today, he scored 117 centuries in first-class matches, including 37 double centuries. He scored 8926 runs in Sheffield Shield matches, for an average of 110 and captained Australia for 12 years, with a Test match average of 99.94 runs. His massive scores led to the "bodyline" tactic used by England in the 1932-33 Tests, in which the ball was used to intimidate batsmen.

Donald Bradman in action.

SOME NOTABLE ACHIEVERS IN AUSTRALIAN SPORTS

Allan Border (1955-), cricketer
John (Jack) Brabham (1926-), racing car driver and designer
Donald Bradman (1908-), cricketer
Haydon Bunton (1911-56), Australian Rules footballer
Roy Cazaly (1893-1963), Australian Rules footballer
Ron Clarke (1937-), runner
Kay Cottee (1954-), solo sailor
Margaret Court (1942-), tennis player
Bart Cummings (1927-), racehorse trainer
Les Darcy (1895-1917), boxer
Herb Elliott (1938-), runner
Jeff Fenech (1964-), boxer
Dawn Fraser (1937-), swimmer
Wayne Gardner (1959-), motor cyclist
Shane Gould (1951-), swimmer
Geoff Hunt (1948-), squash player
Marjorie Jackson (1931-), runner
Rod Laver (1938-), tennis player
Dennis Lillee (1949 -), cricketer
Walter Lindrum (1898-1960), billiards player
Dean Lukin (1960-), weight-lifter
Heather Mackay (1941-), squash player
Dally Messenger (1883-1959), Rugby League footballer
Decima Norman (1910-83), athlete
Greg Norman (1955-), golfer
Hubert Opperman (1904-96), cyclist
Bobby Pearce (1904-76), sculler
Phar Lap (NZ) (1926-32), racehorse

Kieren Perkins (1973-), swimmer
Jimmy Pike (1892-1969), jockey
Ingo Renner (1940-), glider pilot
Murray Rose (1939-), swimmer
Bill Roycroft (1915-), horse rider
Kerry Saxby (1962-), walker
Shirley Strickland (1925-), runner
Kenneth Warby (1939-), speedboat racer

Beatrice Kerr, a champion swimmer, in 1906.

FACTS

▶ After Australia won the Test series in England in 1882, *The Sporting Times* published an obituary of English cricket. A bail was cremated and its ashes became a symbol of future Tests.

▶ The first Australian Rugby Union team to tour overseas changed its name from the Rabbits to the Wallabies on the ship. Its 25 wins included a gold medal at the 1908 Olympics. Fourteen team members defected to Rugby League the following season.

▶ Surfboard riding was introduced to Australia by Hawaiian Duke Kahanomoku in 1915.

▶ Australia is one of only three countries to have competed at every modern Olympic Games. Best medal score was in Melbourne in 1956 (13 gold, 8 silver, 14 bronze).

▶ The racehorse Phar Lap was foaled in New Zealand. He started 51 times for 37 wins.

Australian all over

The colonial necessity to "make or make do" led to Australians inventing all sorts of things. Some of these inventions, and other things Australians have improved and made use of, are included here.

Driza-bone oilskin coat and Akubra hat are symbols of Australia.

Fly away home

Australia was one of the first countries in the world to make aviation an essential part of everyday life.

In 1889, **Lawrence Hargrave** invented a rotary engine which powered a propeller.

Bert Hinkler first flew in a home-made glider in 1912. In 1928, he flew from London to Darwin in 15 days 12 hours.

Navigator Harry Lyon, pilot Charles Kingsford Smith, co-pilot Charles Ulm and wireless operator Jim Warner with the Southern Cross in 1928.

Charles Kingsford Smith, a World War I flying ace, made record-breaking flights around Australia (1927), from California to Brisbane (1928), across the Tasman Sea to New Zealand (1928) and around the world (1930). His most famous aircraft was a Fokker FVII called *Southern Cross*.

Qantas, the world's second-oldest airline, was started by two ex-World War I pilots, Hudson Fysh and P.J. McGinness, in western Queensland, in 1920.

On the beach

Australia has been a leader in practical swimwear since 1902, when William Gocher tested public decency laws by bathing at Sydney's Manly beach wearing a neck-to-knee woollen costume.

Speedos were launched as "the all-Aussie cossie" in the 1920s. In 1952, a model was ordered to leave the beach at Surfers Paradise, Queensland, for wearing an early Paula Stafford-made bikini.

Bondi, a Sydney beach, was the site of the first Australian surf lifesaving club in 1906. The first surf lifesaving carnival was held at another Sydney beach, Manly, in 1908.

Lyster Ormsby, captain of the Bondi Club, invented the portable lifesaving reel, used to haul lifesaver and distressed swimmer back from the surf. One of the first to be rescued in this way, in 1907, was a boy called Charlie Smith, later famous as Sir Charles Kingsford Smith, aviator.

SOME AUSTRALIAN INVENTIONS

- The first **pre-paid postage** system in world, in use in Sydney in 1838.
- The use of **refrigeration**, in James Harrison's 1856 ice factory on the Barwon River.
- The **billy**, originally made from a jam or golden syrup tin for use over a campfire.
- **Granny Smith** apples, first eaten in 1868.
- The **kelpie sheep dog**, bred by the King brothers after 1870.
- Wolseley and Austin's **shearing machine**, developed in 1877, in use by 1888.
- Aboriginal athlete Bobby McDonald's first use of the runner's **crouch start** in 1884.
- The **electric drill** in 1889.
- The **radial rotary aeroplane engine**
- The **blue-heeler cattle dog** appeared 1890.
- **Flotation**, an ore-recovery process devised by Charles Potter at Broken Hill in 1900.
- **Surf lifesaving clubs** and **lifesaving reel.**
- **Spun-concrete pipes**, invented and developed by Walter Hume in 1910.
- The **armoured tank**, designed by Adelaide engineer Lance de Mole in 1912.
- The **totalisator** for betting on horse races, invented by George Julius, later Chairman of the *CSIRO, in use by 1917.
- **Aspro**, developed in 1915, when imports of German aspirin stopped during WWI.
- A.C. Howard's **rotary hoe**, 1912.
- The **mobile home**, created when SA's Pop Kaisler built a house on his 1924 Dodge car.
- The **pedal wireless**, invented by Alf Traeger at the request of Dr John Flynn in 1926.
- The **Flying Doctor Service**, established in 1928, by John Flynn.
- The first **"ute"**, made in 1934 after a farmer asked for a vehicle to take the family to church on Sunday and the pigs to market on Monday.
- The **pavlova**, created in Perth in 1935 for the Russian ballerina Anna Pavlova.
- Ted Both's 1937 **portable iron lung**.

- Ted Both also invented a **humidicrib** for premature babies and the **electric scoreboard** used at the 1956 Olympics.
- The **development of penicillin** (first discovered in 1928 by Fleming) as an antibiotic, by Howard Florey and his team.
- The **Owen sub-machine gun**, submitted to the army by E. Owen in 1939.
- The world's first **pre-mixed concrete** business, Ready-Mixed, in 1939.
- **Antivenoms** to treat snake- and spider-bite.
- Discovery of the **link between German measles and birth defects.**
- Ken Gaunt's **sugar-cane harvester**, 1956.
- **Sirotherm** technique for purifying water.
- **Interscan**, a landing system used at airports worldwide, devised by CSIRO in 1972.
- Ralph Sarich's **orbital car engine**, 1971.
- **Human reproduction technology** which has resulted in the birth of some 20 000 babies.
- The cardboard and plastic **wine cask,** 1965.
- The **"black box"** which records flight data on aircraft, now used for disaster analysis.
- **Indoor cricket**, in Perth, WA, in 1978.
- The ***bionic ear,** first developed by Dr Graeme Clark in 1978.
- The **Super Sopper**, invented by Gordon Withnall to dry flooded sporting areas.
- The **surgical stapling gun.**
- The **Siroset** process which pleats fabric.
- The **split nut**, which can withstand greater tensions than a one-piece nut.
- **Fibreglass sail battens, scanning sonars** and **winged keels** for ocean boat racing.
- **Sirotem** which detects below-surface ores.
- **Computer-based betting** systems.
- Techniques and tools such as **"gene shears"**, which allow scientists to handle living plant and animal material at the level of its tiniest particles.
- The **nanomachine**, which can detect and analyse a minute amount of a substance.

An Australian ute and Australian cattle-dogs.

Surf lifesavers and a surf lifesaving reel.

1801 William Redfern first doctor to qualify.

1804 First small pox vaccinations in Sydney.

1847 Ether used as anaesthetic by Dr Pugh in Launceston.

1850 First record of measles in Australia.

1863 Medical school founded in Melbourne.

1876 Dr Bancroft reveals mosquitoes spread disease.

1890 Dr Constance Stone first female doctor.

1896 Dr Woods uses X-rays to treat cancer.

1902 Realised that fleas carry bubonic plague from rats to humans.

1921 Commonwealth Serum Laboratories established.

1938 Red Cross begins blood-transfusions.

1940s development of antibiotics. Research into birth defects.

1948 Campaign against tuberculosis begins.

1956 Salk vaccine for poliomyelitis available.

1961 Dr William McBride links birth defects and thalidomide.

1968 First liver and heart transplants.

1971 Campaign against German measles.

1980 First "test-tube" baby born in Melbourne.

1983 First known AIDS death in Australia.

1982 First bionic ear transplant.

1984 World's first baby from frozen embryo born in Melbourne.

The human heritage

For every "newsmaker" shown here, there have been large numbers of people, organisations and events which have contributed to the Australia of today. Their existence has influenced the lives of others for better or for worse and they have provided material for newspapers, magazines, books, plays and films.

SOME NEWSMAKERS

ANZAC, name taken from initials of WWI Australian and New Zealand Army Corps

ACTU Australian Council of Trade Unions

ARCHIBALD, Jules (1856-1919), founder of *The Bulletin* journal

BANKS, Joseph (1743-1820), naturalist

BARAK, William (1824-1903), Aboriginal spokesman and artist

BARTON, Edmund (1849-1920), politician

BARWICK, Garfield (1903-97), Chief Justice

BASS, George (1771-1803?), explorer

BATES, Daisy (1863-1951), welfare worker with Aborigines

BENNELONG (1764?-1813), Aboriginal representative

BHP, Broken Hill Proprietary, mining company formed 1885

BLIGH, William (1754-1817), navigator, governor of NSW

BLAMEY, Thomas (1884-1951), soldier

BOROVANSKY, Edouard (1902-59), ballet *entrepreneur

BOYD FAMILY, artistic and literary family

BRADMAN, Donald (1908-), cricketer

BULLETIN, THE, a weekly journal founded 1880

BURNET, Macfarlane (1899-1985), medical scientist

BUSHRANGERS, bush-living law-breakers

BUSSELL, Grace (1860-1935), shipwreck heroine

CHAFFEY BROTHERS, irrigation specialists

CHIFLEY, Joseph (1885-1951), politician, Prime Minister

CHISHOLM, Caroline (1808-77), activist for female immigrants

CLARK, Manning (1915-91), historian

CLARKE, Marcus (1846-81), novelist

CLUNIES ROSS, Ian (1899-1959), scientist

COBB & CO., coaching firm founded in 1853

COLES, George (1885-1977), businessman

CONDER, Charles (1868-1909), painter

COOK, James (1728-79), navigator, mapmaker

COWAN, Edith (1861-1932), politician

CSIRO, Commonwealth Scientific and Industrial Research Organisation, founded 1949

CURTIN, John (1885-1945), politician, Prime Minister

CWA, Country Women's Association, founded 1922

HENRY LAWSON

IL

CYCLONE TRACY devastated Darwin 1974

DAINTREE, Richard (1851-78), geologist

DAMPIER, William (1652?-1715), mariner

DAVIS, Arthur (Steele Rudd) (1868-1935), writer

DEAKIN, Alfred (1856-1919), politician, Prime Minister

DENNIS, C.J. (1876-1938), poet

DOBELL, William (1899-1970), painter

EUREKA REBELLION (1854), conflict on Victorian goldfields

EVATT, Herbert (1894-1965), politician

EYRE, Edward (1815-1901), explorer

FARRER, William (1845-1906), wheat-breeder

FLINDERS, Matthew (1774-1814), navigator

FLOREY, Howard (1898-1968), scientist

FLYNN, John (1880-1951), founder Flying Doctor Service

FORREST, John (1847-1918), explorer and politician

FRASER, Malcolm (1930-), politician, Prime Minister

GIBBS, May (1877-1969), writer and artist

GILL, S.T. (1818-80), painter

GILMORE, Mary (1865-1962), writer

GLOVER, John (1767-1849), painter

GOLDSTEIN, Vida (1869-1949), feminist, writer

GORDON, Adam Lindsay (1833-70), poet

GRAINGER, Percy (1882-1961), musician

GREAT DEPRESSION (1929-1933), time of economic hardship and high unemployment

GREENWAY, Francis (1777-1837), architect

GREER, Germaine (1939-), feminist, writer

GRIFFIN, Walter Burley (1876-1937), landscape architect

HARGRAVE, Lawrence (1850-1915), aviation pioneer

HARTOG, Dirk (dates unknown), mariner

HARVESTER JUDGEMENT set men's basic wage, 1907

HASLUCK, Paul (1905-93), politician, Governor-General

HAWKE, Robert (1929-), politician, Prime Minister

HEAGNEY, Muriel (1885-1974), feminist, trade unionist

HEIDELBERG SCHOOL, a group of Australian artists painting in the 1880s

HEINZE, Bernard (1894-1982), musician

HINKLER, Bert (1892-1933), pilot

HUGHES, William (1862-1952), politician, Prime Minister

KELLY, Ned (1855-80), bushranger

KINGSFORD-SMITH, Charles (1897-1935), pilot

LALOR, Peter (1827-89), rebel, politician

LAMBING FLAT RIOTS (1860-61), clashes between Europeans and Chinese diggers in NSW

LAND RIGHTS, the land and political rights of Aborigines

LAWSON, Henry (1867-1922), writer, poet

LAWSON, Louisa (1848-1920), feminist, writer

LEICHHARDT, Ludwig (1813-48?), explorer

LIGHT, William (1786-1839), Adelaide planner

LINDSAY FAMILY, artistic and literary family

LYONS, Enid (1897-1981), politician

MACARTHUR, John (1767-1834), pastoralist

McCUBBIN, Frederick (1855-1917), painter

MACKELLAR, Dorothea (1885-1968), poet

McKILLOP, Mary (1842-1909), founder of Sisterhood of St Joseph

MAWSON, Douglas (1882-1958), geologist, explorer

MELBA, Nellie (1861-1931), singer

MENZIES, Robert (1894-1978), politician

MITCHELL, Thomas (1792-1855), surveyor and explorer

MONASH, John (1865-1931), soldier

MYER, Sidney (1878-1934), businessman

NAMATJIRA, Albert (1902-59), painter

NOLAN, Sidney (1917-92), painter

Caroline Chisholm, who promoted emigration to Australia, looked after female immigrants and established schools. She was 44 when this portrait was made.

NUCLEAR TESTS, held by British Government 1952-63

OLYMPIC GAMES, in Melbourne 1956, in Sydney 2000

ORD RIVER IRRIGATION SCHEME, Kimberley, WA, in 1960

OVERLAND TELEGRAPH LINE, completed 1872

PARKES, Henry (1815-96), politician

PATERSON, A.B. (Banjo) (1864-1941), poet

PHILLIP, Arthur (1738-1814), first Governor NSW

PRITCHARD, Katharine (1883-1969), writer

PRESTON, Margaret (1875-1963), painter

QANTAS, airline founded in 1920

REIBEY, Mary (1777-1855), businesswoman

ROBERTS, Tom (1856-1931), painter

ROWAN, Ellis (1848-1922), botanist, painter

SNOWY MTS HYDRO-ELECTRIC SCHEME, engineering feat begun 1949 completed 1972

SPENCE, Catherine (1825-1910), writer

STEAD, Christina (1902-83), writer

STREETON, Arthur (1867-1943), painter

STUART, John McDouall (1815-66), explorer

STURT, Charles (1795-1869), explorer

SUTHERLAND, Joan (1926-), singer

TRUGANINI (1812?-1876), Aboriginal intermediary

UNAIPON, David (1872-1967), Aboriginal inventor

WENTWORTH, William (1790-1872), explorer, politician

WHITE, Patrick (1912-90), writer

WHITLAM, Gough (1916-), politician, Prime Minister

William Charles Wentworth, an explorer who became a colonial statesman.

Australian icons

A few of the things which Australians, and overseas visitors as well, consider typical of Australia

Uluru is becoming higher, as weathering lowers the surrounding plains.

Uluru

Around 600 million years ago, the earth's surface was squeezed upwards to form Central Australia's Petermann Ranges. Rivers rushing down these ranges dropped boulders and sand, which were pressure-cooked into sandstone. Uluru was left exposed when softer surrounding rocks weathered away. In 1873, William Gosse was the first European to see the rock, which rises 348 metres from the plain and extends three kilometres underground.

Australia's coat of arms

The first Commonwealth Coat of Arms, featuring kangaroo and emu supporting a cross of St George, was granted by King Edward VII in 1908. A new device, in which kangaroo and emu support a shield containing the badges of the six States, and which features branches of wattle and a scroll bearing the word "Australia", was approved by King George V in 1912. The identifying colours of the coat of arms are gold and blue.

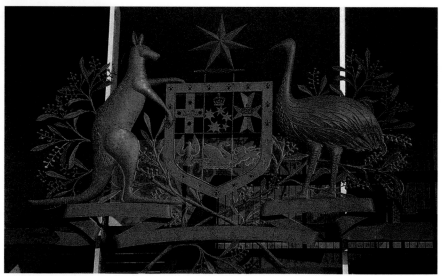

The Commonwealth Coat of Arms, on the High Court of Australia.

The Sydney Harbour Bridge and Sydney Opera House.

Sydney Bridge and Opera House

Francis Greenway first proposed building a bridge from Dawes Point to the north shore of Sydney Harbour in 1815. In 1923, NSW engineers and an English construction firm began the task. The two sections were joined on 19 August 1930 and NSW Premier Jack Lang officially opened the bridge on 19 March 1932. Danish architect Joern Utzon designed Sydney's Opera House, which stands on Bennelong Point and was completed in 1972. The first performance took place in it in 1973.

The Twelve Apostles on one of the world's most scenic coastlines.

The Twelve Apostles

Victoria's south-western coastline fights a losing battle with the surging waves of the Southern Ocean. Wave-borne sand and stones batter the bases of cliffs, undermining them until they collapse, leaving pillars of harder stone standing offshore. Port Campbell National Park includes many wave-cut islands and stacks. The first stage of the Great Ocean Road, which borders much of this coastline, was begun by returned servicemen in 1919 and opened in 1932. The road was completed in the 1980s.

The didgeridoo is played at traditional Aboriginal ceremonies.

The didgeridoo

The didgeridoo is a musical instrument originally used by the Aborigines of Northern Australia for ceremonies and entertainment. A natural trumpet, it is usually made from a tree branch hollowed by termites and decorated with traditional patterns. A player must master difficult "circular breathing" techniques so that the deep droning note is continuous. An expert "didg" player can imitate sounds ranging from bird calls and animal cries to traffic noises and human speech.

Saltwater Crocodile

The first crocodile-like reptiles appeared on earth about 240 million years ago. They were so successful as water-living predators that today's crocodiles have changed little in form. The group to which today's crocodiles belong can be traced back 160 million years. By 1971, hunters had reduced northern Australia's crocodile population to the point where they had to be protected by law. Today wild numbers have built up again and the species is also farmed.

A Saltwater Crocodile basks in the sunshine.

The Pinnacles

For much of the past million years, the west of Australia was covered by a shallow sea. The sand dunes on the shores of this sea became covered with plants. Rainwater trickled through the surface sand, following the paths of plant roots and carrying dissolved minerals which hardened into columns. Wind blew away the sand between columns to leave the Pinnacles which today stand in Nambung National Park, WA. (Some may have been formed as recently as 80 000 years ago.)

Wind-driven sand has sculpted the Pinnacles into their present shapes.

A female Koala has only one young at a time.

The Koala

As Australia gradually became drier in the millions of years after breaking away from Gondwana, rainforest-living Koalas adapted to a diet of eucalypt leaves. Aborigines hunted Koalas; Europeans slaughtered them for their skins; the ones that remain are protected.

The Ghost Gum is a tree of Australia's arid regions.

Eucalypt trees

There are at least 455 different types of eucalypts, and they include about 95% of Australia's forest trees. They include gums, bloodwoods, ironbarks, boxes, mallees and stringybarks and grow in many habitats.

The Murray River spreads over its floodplain.

The Murray River

The Murray River rises in the Australian Alps and flows 2530 km to the Southern Ocean at Encounter Bay, SA. It forms the border between New South Wales and Victoria and irrigates over 1.25 million hectares of farmland. Its tributaries include the Murrumbidgee and Darling Rivers.

The male Red Kangaroo is the largest living marsupial.

Kangaroos

Kangaroo ancestors may have lived in trees, but as Australia became drier most adapted to living on the ground and eating grass. The Red and the Grey Kangaroos are plentiful, but many small species are now rare and a few are extinct.

Glossary & Acknowledgements

Acre. A measure of land, about 4050 sq. metres.

Alluvial gold. Gold found in mud, sand and other material in a river bed.

Amazon. A legendary female warrior.

Ambassador. One nation's representative to another.

Annulled. Cancelled.

Anthropologist. Someone who studies human societies and customs.

Archaeologist. Someone who studies things people have made and used in the past.

Archipelago. A group of islands.

Autobiography. The story of a person's life written by the person.

Barometer. A weather-forecasting instrument which measures pressure of atmosphere.

Bends. A disease caused by gas bubbles in blood expanding when diver rises to the surface too quickly.

Biography. The story of a person's life told by another.

Bionic. Mechanical, behaving like part of a human body.

Botanist. Someone who studies plants.

British Admiralty. The department running the British Navy.

Bushranger. A robber living in the bush.

Careened. Turned ship on side for repair or cleaning.

Combine harvester. A machine that harvests grain and separates it from other matter in one operation.

Compass. A navigation instrument which shows true north.

Conscription. Compulsory enlistment into armed service.

Consecrated. Declared to be a sacred place.

Constitution. A set of principles according to which a country is governed, or document listing them.

Contraceptive. Something which prevents pregnancy.

Cremation. The disposal of a corpse using fire.

CSIRO. Commonwealth Scientific and Industrial Research Organisation.

Cultured pearl. A pearl produced after a foreign body is placed inside an oyster, which covers it with pearl shell.

Depression. A period of low economic well-being.

Dugout canoe. A vessel made from a hollowed tree-trunk.

Entrepreneur. Someone who makes a business or event happen.

Erosion. The wearing away of the Earth's surface by wind, rain, etc.

Extinct. No longer in existence.

Forgery. The creation of a false document passed off as the work of another person.

Gallon. A measure of liquid equal to 4.546 litres.

Geologist. Someone who studies the earth's crust.

Guerilla tactics. Fighting in small, independently acting groups using methods suited to the terrain.

Guinea. A British gold coin first made for Africa trade but no longer used.

Habitat. The natural home of a plant or animal.

Hurling. An Irish game similar to hockey.

Lode. A vein of metal ore.

Mammal. A warm-blooded, fur-bearing animal which feeds its young on milk.

Marsupial. A mammal whose young ones complete their pre-natal development outside their mother's body.

Martial law. Law imposed by military forces.

Megafauna. Unusually large animals which were extinct in Australia by 20 000 years ago.

Merino sheep. A breed of sheep noted for fine wool.

Midshipman. A naval rank above cadet.

Ming Dynasty. The rulers of China, 1368–1644.

Monitor lizard. A fast-moving lizard with forked tongue.

Monument. Something, usually a structure, that reminds people of an event or human actions.

Mosaic. Artwork made by joining many pieces of stone or other substance together to make a picture or pattern.

Obituary. Notice of death.

Ozone. A form of oxygen present in atmosphere.

Panning. A method of washing earth leaving gold behind.

Predator. An animal which eats other animals.

Prototype. A trial model or first version of something.

Racist. Someone whose judgements of people are influenced by their race.

Rail gauge. The distance between the rails of a railway line.

Referendum. A process for putting a political question to the electors for a vote. A YES vote by a majority of voters in a majority of States is needed to change the Australian Constitution.

Reptile. An animal whose temperature remains much the same at the temperature of its surroundings.

Reservoir. A place where reserve supplies are held.

Roaring Forties. Strong winds blowing from west to east around the Earth between 40 and 50 degrees of latitude.

Royal Marines. British troops serving on land or sea.

Royalties. Money paid for the right to use something invented or owned by someone else.

Shilling. Former unit of money; 12 pence.

Silesia. Former East German State.

Smelting. Extracting metal from ore by melting.

Subsidies. Money granted by a govern-ment to keep down the price of goods.

Supernatural. Beyond the natural.

Superphosphate. Fertiliser made from treated phosphate rock.

Syndicate. People forming a group to make profit.

Treason. The betrayal of the ruler of a nation by a subject.

Trepang. A marine animal that does not have a spine, sometimes called *sea cucumber*. Cooked as food.

Typhoid. Highly infectious illness, having fever and red spots on the skin as some of its symptoms.

Acknowledgements

PHOTOGRAPHY: Steve Parish (uncredited photographs). Other illustrations are marked with initials, and thanks are due to the following for supplying illustrations and granting permission to reproduce:

AHM Aviation Heritage Museum, NT
APL Australian Picture Library (p. 13 Joe Mann; p. 43 John Carnemoll)
APLC Australian Parliamentary Library Collection
BL Battye Library (p. 36, 209353P; p. 44, 5836P courtesy Royal Western Australian Historical Society, Inc.)
BW Belinda Wright
EL courtesy Eric Lindgren
IL Image Library, State Library of New South Wales
IM Ian Morris
JOL Collection: John Oxley Library, Brisbane

ML Marie Lochmann, Lochmann Transparencies
NLA National Library of Australia
PAA Picturesque Atlas of Australasia, Vols 1–3, courtesy Allan Fox (+ inside front & back covers; pp. 2, 3; 33 insets; portraits p. 45)
PES Pat Slater
PH Phillip Hayson
PS Peter Slater (Gould painting p. 51 courtesy Peter Slater)
QM The Queensland Museum
SB Stanley Breeden
SLV State Library of Victoria
STL Sport, the Library (p. 4 Glenn Allen; p. 70 David Callow)
TMAG Tasmanian Museum and Art Gallery
WAMM Western Australian Maritime Museum
Maps pp. 14, 46 based on maps prepared by MAPgraphics, Brisbane, Qld

Map

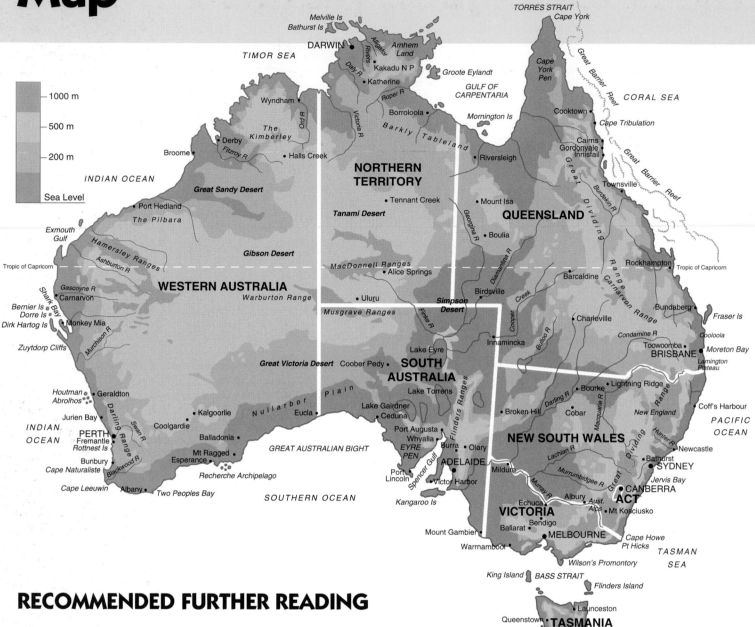

RECOMMENDED FURTHER READING

ABORIGINAL AND TORRES STRAIT ISLANDER COMMISSION, 1991. *Aboriginal Australia*.

ADAM-SMITH, PATSY, 1981. *Outback Heroes*. Lansdowne Press, Sydney.

BASSETT, JAN, 1996. *The Oxford Illustrated Dictionary of Australian History*. Oxford University Press, Melbourne.

CANNON, MICHAEL, 1978. *Australia in the Victorian Age*, Vols 1-3. Nelson, Melbourne.

CANNON, MICHAEL, 1987. *The Exploration of Australia*. Readers Digest, Sydney.

CLARK, MANNING, 1992. *A Short History of Australia, illustrated edition*. Penguin Books, Australia.

DENNIS, GREY, MORRIS & PRIOR, 1995. *The Oxford Companion to Australian Military History*. Oxford University Press, Melbourne.

DE VRIES, SUSANNA, 1995. *Strength of Spirit: Pioneering Women of Achievement*. Millennium Books, Sydney.

LAIDLAW, R, 1989. *The Land They Found*. Macmillan, Melbourne.

LUCK, PETER, 1992. *Australian Icons*. William Heinemann, Melbourne.

OLDS, MARGARET (ED.), 1995. *Australia Through Time*. Random House Australia, Sydney.

ROSS, JOHN (ED.), 1993. *The Chronicle of Australia*. Chronicle Australasia, Melbourne.

STATHAM, P. (ED.), *The Origins of Australia's Capital Cities*. Cambridge University Press, Sydney.

First published in Australia by Steve Parish Publishing Pty Ltd
PO Box 2160 Fortitude Valley BC Queensland 4006
© copyright Steve Parish Publishing Pty Ltd, 1997

ISBN 1-875932-37-2

Printed in Hong Kong
Editing and design by Steve Parish Publishing, Australia
Colour separations by Steve Parish Publishing, Australia